Praise for *The Sales Reset*

Heart and skill are not opposites. In *The Sales Reset*, Wesleyne Whittaker shows how belief before behavior transforms not just results but relationships. Salespeople will discover a practical path to sustainable success built on authenticity, consistency, and resilience.

Shari Levitin | Top 50 Keynote Speaker Worldwide and Author of Bestselling *Heart and Sell*

The greatest obstacle we face in sales is ourselves. When we master ourselves we can master anything. Here's the solution we've all been looking for, *The Sales Reset*. Caution! Do not read this book without a highlighter in hand....it's that good!

Mark Hunter | International Sales Speaker and Author of *A Mind for Sales*

The Sales Reset is the book outbound teams have been waiting for. Wesleyne Whittaker gives sales professionals a mindset first framework that anchors activity in authenticity, consistency, and process. She shows how to prospect with purpose, lead with discovery, and turn effort into real, repeatable revenue. This is a guide every sales leader should put in the hands of their team.

Leslie Venetz | USA Today Best Selling Author, *Profit Generating Pipeline*

Wesleyne not only brings authenticity and connection into every page, but she elevates what I have always believed: Show Me You Know Me is not just a mantra, it is the heart of modern selling. This book gives readers a practical guide that is a relief to every other sales book filled with fluff and dated salesy tactics.

Samantha McKenna | LinkedIn Top Voice and Founder of #samsales Consulting

As someone who has spent my career educating and mentoring the next generation of sales leaders, I found *The Sales Reset* to be exactly the kind of book our field needs. Wesleyne Whittaker connects mindset, process, and authenticity in a way that makes complex concepts simple, actionable, and sustainable. This is not just another tactics book. It is a framework that helps students and professionals alike build confidence, resilience, and real-world results. Every sales educator, leader, and practitioner should have a copy on their desk.

Dr. Lenita Davis | Executive Director of UWEC Professional Sales and Sales Management Program

The Sales Reset is the guide every leader in distribution has been waiting for. Wesleyne Whittaker shows how to align belief and behavior to create teams that are resilient, consistent, and customer focused. Her mindset first framework connects process and people in a way that transforms operations from transactional to strategic. This book is a blueprint for leading through complexity with clarity and building value that endures.

David Potts | Director National Data Center Business, Graybar Electric

The Sales Reset speaks directly to the heart of what leadership and education can accomplish when belief and action are aligned. Wesleyne Whittaker crafts a mindset first framework that bridges the gap between theory and practice, showing how process can empower people to lead with clarity, purpose, and impact. Moreover, Wesleyne demonstrated the joy in selling. This book is a must read for anyone committed to elevating both learning and doing, especially in complex fields like pharmaceutical manufacturing.

Marlow Hicks | Managing Director, Iowa Bioscience Innovation Facility

I've had the privilege of working closely with Wesleyne Whittaker as both a consultant and a trusted partner in my business. What sets her apart is not just her deep expertise in sales, but the way she reshapes how people think about selling altogether. *The Sales Reset* captures that rare ability to move teams beyond scripts and surface-level tactics, and into a mindset of belief, resilience, and authentic connection. BELIEF Selling™ isn't theory, it's a framework that sticks, builds consistency, and transforms revenue into something durable. This is a book I would recommend to any executive who wants their sales organization to stop chasing fragile wins and start building lasting growth.

Erica Parks, CPA, MBA | President & CEO, CBE Companies

The Sales Reset

Forget the Scripts
Trust Yourself
Win Consistently

WESLEYNE WHITTAKER

The Sales Reset © Copyright 2025 Wesleyne Whittaker

All rights reserved. No part of this publication may be reproduced, distributed or transmitted in any form or by any means, including photocopying, recording, or other electronic or mechanical methods, without the prior written permission of the publisher, except in the case of brief quotations embodied in critical reviews and certain other noncommercial uses permitted by copyright law.

BELIEF Selling™ is a trademark of Transformative Business Solutions, LLC. Unauthorized use is strictly prohibited.

Although the author and publisher have made every effort to ensure that the information in this book was correct at press time, the author and publisher do not assume and hereby disclaim any liability to any party for any loss, damage, or disruption caused by errors or omissions, whether such errors or omissions result from negligence, accident, or any other cause.

Adherence to all applicable laws and regulations, including international, federal, state, and local governing professional licensing, business practices, advertising, and all other aspects of doing business in the US, Canada, or any other jurisdiction, is the sole responsibility of the reader and consumer.

Neither the author nor the publisher assumes any responsibility or liability whatsoever on behalf of the consumer or reader of this material. Any perceived slight of any individual or organization is purely unintentional.

The resources in this book are provided for informational purposes only and should not be used to replace the specialized training and professional judgment of a health care or mental health care professional.

Neither the author nor the publisher can be held responsible for the use of the information provided within this book. Please always consult a trained professional before making any decision regarding treatment of yourself or others.

For more information, email gethelp@transformedsales.com

ISBN: 979-8-9999521-3-4 - eBook
ISBN: 979-8-9999521-2-7 - Paperback
ISBN: 979-8-9999521-1-0 - Hardcover

Before You Dive In...

Get your free BELIEF Selling™ Toolkit, created to help you put the strategies from *The Sales Reset* into action immediately.

I see you.

You're here because you want more:

More confidence in your sales conversations,

More consistency in your results,

More control over your success.

I know what it's like to put in the work and still feel like you're spinning your wheels; to wonder if you're saying the right thing, reaching out to the right people, or handling objections in the best way.

That's why I put this together. It's not just a companion, but a practical resource to help you build belief and execute with clarity.

Grab the full downloadable version at **www.yoursalesreset.com**

What's Inside the Toolkit:

- ✓ **BELIEF Affirmations**
  Center your mindset before prospecting, presenting, or leading. These affirmations are your mental reset button when doubt creeps in.

- ✓ **BELIEF Journal Prompts**
  Weekly prompts to help you process what you're learning and how you're growing. This is how you stay grounded while your results rise.

- ✓ **Writing Your Story Worksheet**
  Connect your personal story to your strength in sales. Reflect on the moments that shaped you and carry that resilience into your next call.

- ✓ **Funnel Quick Reference Guide**
  Your full sales process at a glance. No more second-guessing what's next. Every stage mapped, every mindset reset.

- ✓ **Funnel Reset Worksheet**
  Walk through each funnel stage and uncover the limiting belief that might be holding you back. Then flip the script and take aligned action.

- ✓ **SWOT Analysis Worksheet**
  See your company through the eyes of your customer. Get clear on your strengths and blind spots so you can sell with confidence.

- ✓ **Competitive Analysis Worksheet**
  Assess your competitors using real data, not guesses. Learn where you win and how to claim your lane.

- ✓ **Pain-Problem-Impact Mapping Worksheet**
  Tie what your buyer says to what's really going on and why it matters. This is how you sell the solution, not the symptom.

- ✓ **Prospecting Cheat Sheet**
  Use the 3 Pillars of Intentional Outreach to stop guessing and start connecting. Whether you're networking, educating, or going direct, this keeps you focused.

- ✓ **Warm Emailing Guide**
  Cold emails that don't feel cold. Use this framework to open doors, build trust, and start better conversations.

- ✓ **DIVE DEEP Discovery™ Framework**
  Discovery shouldn't feel like interrogation. These are the questions that create clarity, not pressure for you and your buyer.

- ✓ **Proposal One-Pager Planning Guide**
    Stop sending quotes and hoping. Use this to prep your one-pager with purpose, then guide your buyer toward a confident decision.

This toolkit isn't just a download, it's your daily anchor.

Come back to it often, trust yourself deeply, and remember you were never meant to sell like everyone else.

You were meant to sell with BELIEF.

Dedication

To every field sales professional who has ever questioned their worth, struggled to hit their numbers, or felt like they were shouting into the void, this book is for you.

To those who refuse to settle for mediocrity, who push past rejection, and who show up every day determined to serve, solve, and succeed: you are the backbone of business, the driving force behind innovation, and the lifeblood of industry.

And to those who have been told they are not "natural" salespeople, who have battled self-doubt, and who are ready to sell in a way that feels authentic and powerful: may this book be the turning point in your journey.

I see you. I believe in you. Now let's go close some deals.

~ Wesleyne Whittaker

Contents

Introduction: Selling Is Not Just About Skills. It's About BELIEF	15
Chapter 1: Entering the Mysterious World of Sales	25
Chapter 2: Why Selling Is About People, Not Products	37
Chapter 3: Winning Starts in Your Mind	51
Chapter 4: From Chaos to Consistency	69
Chapter 5: Building Your Competitive Edge	81
Chapter 6: The Power of the Buying Committee	93
Chapter 7: The Power of Impact: Turning Problems Into Opportunities	107
Chapter 8: Mastering Prospecting: Turning Effort Into Results	119
Chapter 9: Diagnose Before You Prescribe: The Power of Discovery	135
Chapter 10: Stop Selling on Price, Start Selling on Value	149
Chapter 11: Turning Resistance Into Revenue	161
Chapter 12: Mastering Your Territory: From Surviving to Thriving	175
Chapter 13: Bet on Yourself	187
Appendix: Tools to Put BELIEF Selling™ Into Action	191

INTRODUCTION

Selling Is Not Just About Skills. It's About BELIEF

"All that warm, fuzzy stuff you like to talk about will not move the needle, Wesleyne. I need my team to close more business. Better discovery meetings. Faster pitches," Greg said, blunt and to the point. "I've been selling for 25 years. I know the issue. I need you to fix it."

I stayed quiet, letting his words hang in the air.

After a moment, he added, "We're at 85 percent of our goal, and the pipeline is soft. If things don't change, we're not catching up. Maybe prospecting is the problem too. Closing and prospecting. That's what they need."

He leaned back and smiled like he had it figured out.

I returned the smile. "Then why did you call me?"

His confidence cracked. He shifted, his voice softer. "My top rep said... you. He's at 150 percent. The rest? Barely hitting 50. Some, not even 30."

He exhaled. "It's too late to hire. I need this team to turn around, fast. But I don't have time for mindset talk."

Then came a pause. A different kind of silence. The kind that cracks open something deeper.

I leaned in. "Greg, the mindset work is why your top rep is thriving. He's not just selling. He believes in what he's doing. That belief fuels every action."

Eyebrows raised, Greg said, "So... it's not just skills. It's how they think?"

I nodded. "Exactly. Once we shift that, the rest falls into place."

He sat forward, hands on the desk. "Alright, Wesleyne. I'm in."

So who is Wesleyne?

I'm someone who's had to fight to be heard in rooms where I didn't fit the mold. I started out as a chemist, made my way into sales, and built a reputation as a top performer, not because I knew all the tactics, but because I learned how to think differently.

Now I work with field sales teams who are great at what they do but still aren't seeing the results they want. And it's not because they're lazy or unskilled. It's because no one has helped them deal with what's really holding them back.

That's what this book is about. We'll talk about mindset before mechanics, belief before behavior. Because when you fix the root, the results come faster, and they actually stick.

And here's what I've learned after working with hundreds of sales professionals just like Greg: he was right about one very important thing—results matter.

But Greg was missing the bigger picture. Success in sales isn't just about better pitches or faster meetings. It starts with believing that your actions will lead to the results you want. That's where BELIEF Selling™ comes in.

If you want long-term success in sales, you have to shift your belief system. Let's take a deep dive into what that means and why it is critical to your career.

> **Success in sales starts with believing that your actions will lead to the results you want.**

BELIEF Selling™: From Mindset to Mastery

Sales success is not just about having the right script, a perfect pitch, or an endless list of leads. If that were true, every salesperson with a decent playbook would be thriving.

But the reality is that sales is more than just a numbers game. It is a mindset game.

Think about the most successful salespeople you know. What makes them different? It is not just that they prospect more or run better meetings. It is that they think differently about selling. They do not hesitate to reach out to high-value prospects. They do not take rejection personally. They do not get stuck overanalyzing before taking action.

> ***The difference between top performers and struggling salespeople comes down to their BELIEF system.***

The difference between top performers and struggling salespeople comes down to their BELIEF system.

BELIEF Selling™ is built on six pillars.

- Break Barriers—Identify and eliminate the self-limiting beliefs that hold you back.
- Embrace Growth—Replace those barriers with an empowered, growth-oriented way of thinking.
- Learn Skills—Build the skills necessary to execute at the highest level.
- Implement Boldly—Apply what you have learned in real-world sales situations with confidence.
- Execute Consistently—Success is built through repetition.
- Fuel Others—Teaching what you learn cements your mastery and lifts others in the process.

BELIEF Selling™ isn't just a method. It's a shift in how you show up. Most sales training starts with tactics. This starts with you. Your mindset. Your habits. Your ability to execute with confidence and consistency. Because if your beliefs don't align with your actions, the results won't last.

BELIEF Selling™ helps you build the foundation to win from the inside out and keep winning. Each step builds on the one before it. You cannot implement boldly if your mindset is full of doubt. You cannot learn new skills if you are stuck in your old patterns of thinking.

If your beliefs don't align with your actions, the results won't last.

This system is not just a framework. It is the foundation for long-term, sustainable success in sales.

BELIEF Selling™ is for business-to-business sales professionals who are tired of surface-level fixes. You don't need more fluff. You need something that actually sticks. This is for people who are in the field, talking to real clients, managing real pressure, and still showing up every day. You know the numbers matter, but you also know the way you think drives the outcome. This is where you learn to shift that.

Now, let's break it down step by step.

Break Barriers

A barrier is a self-limiting belief, an unhelpful thought that holds you back. These beliefs are often ingrained in you during childhood, so deeply embedded that you accept them as truth without questioning them.

Maybe your parents told you that nothing less than straight A's was acceptable. Then, in seventh grade, you got a B. Despite working hard all semester, attending extra tutoring, and doing dozens of practice problems, Algebra was just tough for you. But instead of acknowledging your effort, your parents scolded and punished you.

At just 12 years old, you internalized the belief, "Without perfection, I will not succeed."

Fast forward to adulthood, and that belief still controls you. You hesitate to take risks because you fear falling short of perfection. That fear holds you back.

Think about it: your parents expected you to be perfect, but in sales, perfection isn't the goal. You might have internalized the idea that if you don't hit the mark every time, you're failing. That belief keeps you from picking up the phone or closing the deal.

Before learning how to prospect more consistently or run more effective discovery meetings, you have to identify and break your opposing beliefs.

You might be surprised to learn that for every sales skill you want to master, there is a belief you must first shatter. This is where we start.

Embrace Growth

You cannot start something new without stopping something old. You cannot start losing weight unless you stop eating junk food. You cannot start paying off debt unless you stop spending recklessly. You can't expect to become a top salesperson if you don't release old habits that are keeping you stuck.

You may have tried to embrace a growth mindset before, only to fall back into old patterns. That is because you never identified and broke the barriers keeping you trapped in a fixed mindset.

Most people want to skip the hard work of dealing with what's really holding them back. They jump straight to the feel-good part of empowerment. But that shortcut will keep you stuck.

And being stuck is beyond frustrating. It's what happens when you start to believe that nothing can change, that your abilities are limited, and that who you are right now is all you'll ever be.

That is a fixed mindset in action.

A growth mindset tells a different story.

It says you can learn. You can stretch. You can get stronger through every challenge.

With a fixed mindset, you attack every problem the same way. You assume what worked in the past will work again. When new ideas seem too difficult, you resist them and stick to what feels safe.

Shifting to a growth mindset requires discomfort. You have to release your attachment to the outcome and focus only on the input.

That input starts with the words you speak to yourself.

Think about it. If your best friend lost a big deal, you would never say, "You suck. Maybe sales is not for you."

Yet, when you lose a deal, what do you tell yourself?

"I am a failure."

"I am not good at this job."

"This only happens to losers, which means I am a loser."

That kind of thinking will keep you stuck. Instead of dwelling on failure, reframe your thoughts.

"I did not win the deal, but I am not a failure."

"One lost deal does not mean I am bad at my job."

Changing the conversation in your head is the first step to elevating your mindset.

Learn Skills

Now that your mind is free from self-imposed barriers, it is time to build new skills. But here's the truth:

You are not just learning techniques; you are learning how to trust yourself enough to use them. Most salespeople want to skip ahead to the skills section. That feels easier and more productive. But if you haven't dealt with the noise in your head—the doubts, the fears, the habits that keep you stuck—then those techniques will not stick. You won't have the confidence to try them, and you won't have the resilience to keep using them when it gets hard.

Mindset comes first. Belief comes second. Skillset comes third. That order matters. If you try to reverse it, you will keep hitting invisible walls.

Do the inner work first. Build your foundation. Then the skills will have somewhere to land. You are not just here to become a better salesperson; you are here to become the version of yourself who can sell with confidence, clarity, and conviction.

Remember, learning is not just about taking in new information; it is about applying it.

Implement Boldly

Learning without implementation is a waste of time.

Some salespeople see steady growth and consistent wins, while others stay stuck at the same level year after year. What separates them is not talent; it is what they do after learning.

Top performers don't just go through the motions. They stop reading to reflect. They write down the hard questions and actually answer them. They schedule time on their calendars to complete the exercises instead of hoping they'll get to it later. They test the techniques in real conversations and track what works. When they fall short, they circle back, review the material, and adjust. They stay curious, coachable, and committed.

Underperformers rush through the content. They tell themselves they already know it. They skip the exercises. They don't make space to apply the mindset shifts. And when something feels uncomfortable, they return to their old way of selling because it's what's familiar.

You cannot think your way into success; you must act your way into it.

Execute Consistently

Success does not happen overnight. It happens through repetition.

You will not become an expert at active listening the first time you try it. You have to practice, not once nor when it is convenient—but every single day.

The six-figure sales professionals are not winging it. They are sharpening their skills with the same level of intention that athletes bring to training.

> *Success does not happen overnight. It happens through repetition.*

They role-play objections with a peer before their first call.

They listen to their own recordings while driving between appointments.

They reflect on what they could have done better after every conversation.

This kind of practice doesn't just improve your technique; it builds muscle memory, confidence, and control in the moments that matter. That's how they create consistent results. That's how they build six-figure careers.

You will want to skip it.

You will tell yourself you're too busy.

You'll say you already know this.

But knowing is not the same as doing. Elite sales professionals are the ones who execute like their lives depend on it.

So practice your new skills daily, not just when you feel like it.

Champions train through resistance. That's their secret for winning.

Fuel Others

Sales can feel like a solo journey, but the best way to solidify what you have learned is to teach it.

Your learning cycle is not complete until you can explain it to someone else. When you can share your knowledge, answer questions, and coach others, you are not just improving their success; you are cementing your own.

The salespeople who grow the fastest are the ones who take what they have learned and share it.

BELIEF Selling™ is designed to transform every aspect of your sales process, from prospecting to negotiating. But no matter how many books you read or strategies you learn, you will never achieve true mastery if you do not first identify and break the barriers holding you back.

Success starts with stepping into a growth mindset. Without it, new skills will only take you so far.

Learning alone is not enough. If you take in everything from this book but never implement it or consistently practice it, nothing will change. For lasting transformation, you cannot just understand BELIEF Selling™ — you must use it daily.

Each chapter builds on the one before it. This is not a sprint; it is a marathon.

Give yourself time to work through any mindset challenges you face. Take the time to truly absorb each skill and complete the action items at the end of every chapter. Some will take just a few minutes; others may take weeks. That is okay. Growth happens at its own pace.

Elite athletes train for 40 hours a week for a performance that lasts only three hours.

How many hours are you willing to devote each week to becoming an elite salesperson?

CHAPTER 1

Entering the Mysterious World of Sales

As I sit in the airport waiting to board the plane headed to Munich, Germany, my mind starts to wander. I think about the jagged path I took to get to this moment. Ten-year-old Wesleyne never thought that a sales career was even an option. The only options presented to me were being a doctor, lawyer, or engineer. For my entire life, I proudly proclaimed, "When I grow up, I want to be a doctor and a mommy."

My dream of becoming a doctor shifted radically in college. I went from wanting to be a medical doctor to deciding to get my PhD in chemistry. As a chemistry major, I went all in, moving towards my goal. Each summer, I did research shoulder to shoulder with some of the most brilliant minds. During the school year, I would travel around the country and present my research to people a lot smarter than me.

I got good at succinctly presenting the work I completed over the 12 weeks in the summer and answering all the questions thrown my way. I just knew that I had found my calling—doing cutting-edge research and breaking those concepts down in a way that everyone could understand them.

At the beginning of my senior year in college, I applied to numerous PhD programs. I was accepted into every single one of them and received a full scholarship and a monthly stipend throughout my tenure.

One portion of my dream was coming to fruition. I was going to become the doctor I had been proclaiming for the last decade of my life. Dr. Wesleyne Whittaker had such a nice ring to it.

If you are reading this book, you know that my name does not have a doctor in front of it or a PhD behind it. After my first semester of graduate school, I absolutely hated it. It was hard, unfulfilling, and very lonely. I did well that first semester, taking classes like Medicinal Chemistry and achieving a 3.5 GPA. But I just could not envision spending the next six years of my life in that environment.

For the first time ever, I quit. I didn't complete something that I started. I felt like I gave up on my dream and let everyone down in my life who had been rooting for me. I decided to choose my mental health and happiness over my academic abilities, as I had done for the last 15 years of my life.

One thing I knew how to do was be scrappy. Within a month of leaving graduate school, I had a job working as a failure analysis chemist. In my brand-new position, I was responsible for finding out why plastic parts broke when they were being used. I got to test all kinds of stuff, from Styrofoam plates to the inside of coolers to components of cars.

My first real job out of college made my wheels turn daily, and I absolutely loved it. There was never a straight line between the problem and the solutions. I was the person responsible for writing the story in between and presenting it to the salespeople for them to share with our customers.

Each time a salesperson came back from a business trip, I would be eagerly waiting for their updates and what new problems they had for me to solve.

My favorite salesperson was Joe. He would come find me before I could pop into his office. One day, when things were pretty slow in the lab, he grabbed me and updated me on his most recent customer visits.

Joe said, "Thanks for going the extra mile in testing those samples. The plastic inside the coolers kept breaking right around 30°F. The customer noted that when they dropped juices boxed in, nothing happened, but when they added sodas, they would get microcracks."

I shook my head and told him, "As soon as you mentioned that to me, I figured the problem was not the weight of the object but the weight and temperature combined. That's why I ran all of those tests at various temperatures with different weights to assess the true failure point."

Shaking his head in agreement, Joe said, "Since we had so much data, we were able to offer a solution to the client that enabled them to modify the recommended use conditions for the coolers. Because of these changes, they anticipate their warranty claims on that product to decrease by about 75 percent, which will save them millions of dollars this year."

As a twenty-three-year-old, hearing millions of dollars being saved was foreign to me. How could I, a woman with a Bachelor of Science in Chemistry from a small school in Mississippi, have been instrumental in saving a publicly traded company millions of dollars?

What I did wasn't based on my two years working for the company. It was based on the many years I spent working side by side with researchers, asking the right questions to uncover the root cause of an issue, and being tenacious enough to come up with outside-the-box solutions.

I didn't fully realize it yet, but the skills I was building—solving complex problems, translating technical work into actionable insights, and collaborating with others—were already setting me up for a career I never saw coming: sales.

At the time, I thought my life had to fit into a box and was supposed to look a certain way. But life has a way of surprising us, doesn't it?

You might be wondering, "Wait a second, isn't this supposed to be a book about sales?" And yes, it is. But here's the thing: success in sales doesn't start with scripts or strategies. It starts with you: your story, your experiences, and all the lessons you've picked up along the way.

As we move forward, I'm going to show you not only how to crush it in sales but also how to embrace and leverage your unique journey to rise to the top.

Your Story

Most of us didn't grow up dreaming of a career in sales. We stumbled into it, often coming from a completely unrelated field. When we make that leap, we tend to tell ourselves that the skills and experiences we gained in our previous life don't matter anymore. So, we leave those lessons behind, thinking they're irrelevant to what we're stepping into now.

But here's the truth: your story didn't start with your first paycheck. It started long before that—way back in your childhood. When you take a step back and explore why you do the things you do, you uncover the moments that built your grit, your resilience, and your ability to push through challenges.

Let me tell you about Mary.

Fifteen years into her career in field sales, Mary still struggles with the belief that she's not good enough. On paper, she's a pro: experienced, driven, and consistently meeting her goals. But underneath that, there's a quiet voice that questions her worth.

That feeling traces back to her senior year of high school when she failed her final English test. It put her at risk of not graduating with her class. The thought of not walking across the stage, of not being the first in her family to graduate, was devastating. She never talks about it, but that story still lives in the back of her mind.

But here's the thing about Mary. When faced with the possibility of failure, she didn't give up. She advocated for herself, asking her teacher for a retest. And while her classmates were out celebrating, Mary stayed up late every night, poring over her notes, redoing practice problems, and watching every video she could find on the subject. She refused to take no for an answer.

Mary passed the retest and graduated with her class. That moment shaped her. It's where her grit was born. It taught her to push forward no matter how hard things got.

Today, that same grit fuels her in sales, especially when her old belief creeps back in. But until she rewrites that story in her mind, that quiet voice of self-doubt will still show up in the toughest moments—right before a big presentation, during a negotiation, when she is asked to lead a team.

That is why mindset work matters. The stories we carry shape how we show up and what we believe we are capable of.

Mary's story is not unique.

You have one too.

And just like Mary, your story—the challenges you have faced, the moments you thought you couldn't go on but did—has made you who you are today. It's those experiences that make you great at sales. The ability to take a hit, to get back up, and to keep moving forward is the foundation of resilience. And resilience is the foundation of success in sales.

So, don't discount your past. Don't ignore the lessons you've already learned. Those moments, especially the hard ones, are where your strength was built. They're what give you the

> **The ability to take a hit, to get back up, and to keep moving forward is the foundation of resilience.**

edge, the determination, and the confidence to keep showing up, no matter what.

Your Origin Story Isn't Just a Memory. It's Your Superpower.

Mary's story might not resonate with you. Maybe your path has been smooth. You didn't face adversity growing up. You had a stable home, never dealt with rejection, and transitioned into sales without major roadblocks. And for that, I commend you. Truly, I do.

But if that's the case, let me ask you this: why do you still feel like an imposter? Why do you feel like you're not similar enough to your colleagues to succeed?

> *Your origin story isn't just a memory. It's your superpower.*

Here's the thing: we all have an origin story. It's the jagged path of how we started, where we thought we'd be, and where we've ended up. Whether your journey has been turbulent or smooth, there are moments in your life that shaped you—moments that planted the seeds of who you are today.

To move forward, to shatter the glass walls and ceilings holding you back, you need to take a step back. Catalog the pivotal moments in your life. What have they taught you? And more importantly, how can you use those lessons to your advantage?

No Matter Where You Started, Your Story Has Value.

It's the foundation of your strength, your resilience, and your ability to succeed.

The Impact of Sharing Your Story

Let me walk you through some of the biggest lessons I've learned from the experiences I've shared so far:

Lesson 1: Success isn't tied to a single path.

I changed the type of doctor I wanted to be, and that decision taught me a powerful lesson: there are many ways to achieve the same level of success. I learned to focus on what I wanted to achieve, not how I had to get there.

To this day, I set big goals and figure out the "how" as I go. And if the goal shifts along the way, I give myself grace because the road to success is rarely straight.

Lesson 2: The skills you build will show up in unexpected ways.

When I learned to do and present research, I discovered that I was great at identifying what was broken, finding solutions, and explaining them in ways that made sense to everyone. No, I didn't become a PhD chemist like I once thought I would, but those skills laid the foundation for my success in sales. They made me the go-to person in my company whenever a complex problem needed solving.

Lesson 3: Curiosity is a superpower.

I used to pepper salespeople with questions when I was a chemist. I wanted to understand what they did, how they did it, and why. At the time, I had no idea those questions would change my life. But by stepping outside of my comfort zone and staying curious, I realized I didn't want to stay in the lab. I wanted to be in sales.

My love for sales was born because I was willing to ask questions most people in my role didn't.

Writing Your Story

Now it's your turn.

I want you to carve out 20 minutes.

Grab a pen and a blank sheet of paper. Write down every pivotal moment you can remember, whether good or bad. Don't filter. Just flow. There is something magical about writing your thoughts, not typing them.

For those of you who need a little more structure than a blank sheet of paper, go to **www.yoursalesreset.com** and download the free resource guide. You will find a worksheet with prompts for this exercise.

Next, read the list out loud. Yes, you need to hear your own voice speaking your own experiences to you.

You may feel something in your body. That's the power of your voice no longer keeping things tucked away that have shaped the person you have become. You are listening to your story. The integral moments that no one can ever take away from you.

Now that you have your full list, I want you to make a check mark next to the top three that you feel have impacted you the most. This may be hard; take some time to be thoughtful about this.

On a fresh sheet of paper, we will walk through each lesson one at a time. Start with the lesson, then write what you learned and how it has helped propel you forward in the past.

This book is going to challenge you to do things differently. To get the most benefit, you must do the work. There is no easy button. Nothing or no one you can pay to help you achieve a higher level of success.

So, when I ask you to do something, stop and do it.

You may think it's a waste of time, stupid, or my favorite response is "too warm and fuzzy." You don't know me, but I am asking you to trust me. Trust the process.

Now back to our exercise.

As salespeople, we often look in the mirror and question if we have any clue about what we are doing. When the deal you have been working on for six months falls apart at the last minute or you miss your quota by two percent, your self-doubt will creep in.

In those moments, I want you to refer to your list and remind yourself you were made for this. You didn't walk through a fiery storm alone for no reason; that storm showed you how resilient you could be.

You did not max out every credit card you had and move across the country to take that new job because it was a mistake. That move taught you how to depend on yourself and your abilities.

At this point, you have one of three emotions: you are pumped, drained, or ready to put this book back on the shelf.

If you feel pumped, awesome. It only gets better from here. Each chapter will build on itself and provide you with long-term strategies to grow your business.

If you are drained, give yourself grace. It's not easy to walk through difficult moments in our lives and process them fully. Take some time to work through what you uncovered before moving forward.

If you feel done with this book, I'll ask you to give me a few more chapters or go grab a traditional sales book. Most sales books move into tactics immediately. That's not how I roll. My goal is long-term sustainable change, and we won't get there until we break the bondage of the past.

You've walked with me through my story. Thank you for letting me share it with you. Now, it's time to shift focus to your story so that you can see how your own path sets you up for success.

To help you internalize this, let's break the process down using BELIEF Selling™. These are the steps you can take to own your journey and turn it into your superpower in sales.

BELIEF Selling™ in Action: Building a Strong Foundation

B | Break Barriers

- Reflect on the challenges you've overcome and how they've shaped you into the resilient person you are today.
- Let go of the belief that your story doesn't matter in sales. It does.
- Replace the narrative of "I'm not enough" with "My story makes me unforgettable."

E | Embrace Growth

- Own your journey. Embrace it as the foundation of your success, not a detour.
- When doubt creeps in, remind yourself of moments when you faced challenges head-on and came out stronger.
- Affirm yourself with the mindset that you've already proven you can do hard things.

L | Learn Skills

- Identify a skill or lesson from your past that connects to your success today, even if it feels unrelated at first.
- Think about what you've always been naturally good at and find ways to apply that in sales.
- Stay open to new lessons your past experiences can teach you and use them as a resource for growth.

I | Implement Boldly

- Take one part of your story and share it with someone, whether it's a trusted colleague, mentor, or prospect.
- Use your story to build connections and demonstrate your unique perspective in sales conversations.

- Commit to taking action and remember that boldness moves the needle, not perfection.

E | Execute Consistently

- Make it a habit to revisit your story when you need a boost of confidence or motivation.
- Focus on showing up consistently in both your personal and professional development.
- Give yourself grace when things don't go as planned but stay disciplined in your efforts.

F | Fuel Others

- Share your story with someone who might need inspiration or encouragement in their own journey.
- Be intentional about uplifting others and helping them see the value in their own experiences.
- Remember that by sharing what you've learned, you can build deeper connections and foster success for those around you.

You've just taken a moment to reflect on the power your story holds. By now, you should see how the lessons from your past are not just part of who you are; they are the foundation for the salesperson you are becoming. Your story gives you clarity, resilience, and a sense of purpose.

But what happens when the training you are given does not align with the journey you are on? What happens when the tools they hand you do not feel like tools at all?

Remember Wesleyne waiting to board the plane to Germany? The flight was amazing, with wonderful amenities and a comfy seat. When I arrived, I found myself driving on the opposite side of the road to a remote city two hours away from the airport. I showed up with an open mind, ready to be fully trained on what to sell and how to sell it.

Boy, was I mistaken about what to expect during my two weeks in Germany!

Next, we will explore the difference between product training and actual sales training, and why the gap between the two might be holding you back.

CHAPTER 2

Why Selling Is About People, Not Products

"When will I learn how to sell the instruments?" That was my question on day 13 of 14 at the company's headquarters in Germany.

I was confused and frustrated. After 13 days of product training and learning the history of the company, not a single session covered how to actually sell anything.

My trainer's response left me speechless. "We don't teach you that, but the instruments are easy to sell. Just talk about all the features and specifications, and people will buy from you."

His words stunned me. Just talk about the features? That's all it takes to sell a $30K instrument? I nodded, but inside, I knew something was off. I just couldn't place it, so I chose to believe him. After all, he was the mastermind behind designing the instrument, so he surely knew what he was talking about.

Does this sound similar to your onboarding experience? You sit through hours of product training. You learn every detail about features, specs, and SKUs. You figure out how to navigate the CRM, build quotes, and submit reports. But there is one thing no one teaches you—how to actually sell.

This is where the problem starts.

Salespeople are trained to talk about what the product does, not how it solves problems, not how to understand the customer, or how to uncover what really matters. That is why so many reps end up feature dumping. They talk. They pitch. They present. But they never truly connect.

Feature selling is one of the biggest things holding salespeople back. It keeps the conversation surface-level. It makes it harder to earn trust. And it leaves the buyer thinking, "So what?"

Selling is not about proving how much you know. It is about helping the customer feel understood. It is about guiding them to a solution that fits their world. That takes more than product knowledge. It takes real training on how to think, ask, listen, and lead.

Onboarding Without Direction

Eager and full of energy, 25-year-old me came home from Germany and sat at my desk, ready to begin my first official day as a salesperson. I was excited but completely lost.

Working from home, the silence was overwhelming. As a chemist, I was used to structure. My days were predictable. I moved from lab to lab, running tests and analyzing data. I always knew what to do.

Now I found myself unsure how to get started. So I read through the brochures I brought back from Germany and cleaned out my inbox. When I checked the time, it was only 10:30 a.m. I had successfully killed two and a half hours and still had no idea what I was supposed to be doing.

I was the baby sales rep on a team of seasoned pros. The most experienced rep had started his career when I was still in diapers. I wasn't about to start asking people who could be my parents what I should do every day. What if they told my boss I had no clue? I was terrified that I'd be seen as a mistake.

So I did what any new rep in the early 2000s would do. I Googled, "What does a salesperson do every day?"

The first page was filled with advice for door-to-door and insurance sales. I was supposed to dial a phone book? That wasn't going to help me sell $50,000 instruments to labs and chemical plants.

The Harsh Reality of Selling

By the end of my first full day as an actual salesperson, I felt like a complete failure. I had all this product knowledge, but I had no earthly idea how to find people to talk to about how amazing our products were.

On the second day, I met with my manager and felt safe enough to ask how I should find people to sell to. She told me to look at the previous customer base in my territory and set meetings with them. Existing customers are always interested in our new products.

Excited about getting out of the office and talking to people, I set a few meetings for the following week. I was so proud of myself for having a relatively full calendar my second week.

For the rest of that week, I poured over all the product features, wrote notes about why we were better than our competitors, and packed all my brochures into my bag. On Monday morning, I felt ready to conquer the world. I was beyond excited.

That feeling did not last.

I shook the hand of my first client, introducing myself as Wesleyne Whittaker, their new salesperson. I launched into a polished pitch about our new instruments, highlighting all the features and

> *The harsh reality of selling is that most people fail because they were never taught how to truly sell.*

why we were better than the competition. After talking nonstop for fifteen minutes, I finally paused and asked if they had any questions.

They didn't. In fact, they ended the meeting early and said, "That won't be necessary. I am not interested. Please don't contact me again."

What just happened?

I had done everything I was taught to do. I was prepared. I presented confidently. I hit all the talking points.

Still shaken, I walked into my second meeting of the day and got hit by a negative again. This time, the client cut me off mid-pitch and asked, "Did you set this meeting just to sell to me?"

I said yes. That was my job, right?

He said, "I'm not interested. Don't waste my time again."

I left crushed. Two rejections in one day, back-to-back. I felt broken. Like I had failed.

With my head held low and my spirit crushed into a million different pieces, I went back to my home office to reflect on the day. On a scale from one to ten on how that first day in the field went, I would give it a negative five. It was horrendous.

And deep down, I knew something bigger was happening.

I had followed the script: feature dump, competitor bash, and ended by asking for the sale.

But none of it worked.

That's when I realized something needed to change.

My Turning Point

That afternoon, I turned away from my computer and stared at my wall. Everything about sales sucked right now. I was working in a chamber of silence; I had no one to talk to, my customers hated me, and I wasn't selling anything.

I closed my eyes and said, "God, what should I do?" I sat in silence for a nice long time. At some point, Joe, my favorite salesperson, popped into my mind.

I thought about the many hours we spent talking about customers' problems and how it was our job to find the solutions to their problems, not just sell them something new. That's when the lightbulb went off in my head: I was going about this all wrong.

No one cared about my product features or why we were better than the competitors. They cared about themselves, their issues, and how I could help resolve them.

This led me to ask: how could I get people who didn't know me to openly share about their lives? I had no clue, but I decided to try what worked in the past when I was trying to get to the root cause of a customer issue. I would ask questions and let the customer talk.

This, my friends, was the key that allowed me to take my territory, which had only produced $50,000 annually in the previous three years, to generate $500,000 in revenue in 11 months.

Learning What Customers Need

Now, you might be thinking, "Okay, Wesleyne. You had your lightbulb moment. But what did you actually do differently?"

Let me break it down for you.

Step 1: Ask Open-Ended Questions

I didn't walk in with a pitch anymore. I walked in with curiosity. I asked questions that gave the customer space to talk about their world, not mine.

Asking things like:

- What's been your biggest frustration lately?

- What's changed in your process in the last six months?
- What's something you wish your team had more of right now?

Step 2: Be Fully Present

I stopped thinking about what I was going to say next. I stopped obsessing over sounding smart. I just listened. I paid attention to what they were really saying. I looked for their tone, their body language, and the emotions behind their words.

Step 3: Repeat and Clarify

Once they finished talking, I'd say, "So it sounds like you're dealing with [their challenge]. Did I get that right?"

When you repeat back what they said, you show them that you're not just checking a box. You're in it with them.

Step 4: Go Deeper

Sometimes, people talk about the symptom, not the root. It's your job to gently peel that back.

If they say, "We're short on staff," the deeper issue might be burnout or bad systems.

So try asking, "How's that showing up day to day for your team?"

That's where the truth comes out.

Step 5: Let Them Guide The Path Forward

Before I jumped into solutions, I'd ask, "Out of everything we just talked about, what's most important for us to focus on first?"

It's not about forcing your agenda. It's about helping them solve their biggest pain.

This was how I started having real conversations. Not sales calls. Not product pitches. Conversations. And that's when the shift happened.

People started saying yes, not because I talked more, but because I listened better.

I used that hidden skill of being curious that I didn't even know was important.

Starting my second week in sales to this very moment, I introduce myself the same way the first time I meet a client: "Hi, my name is Wesleyne. Thanks for taking the time to meet with me today. I'm here to learn about you. Can you please tell me about yourself?"

> **People started saying yes, not because I talked more, but because I listened better.**

Sometimes they tell me about their kids. And I listen. Because what's on their mind is more important than what's in my pitch.

Your job is to meet your client where they are and follow their lead. Sometimes this means understanding that their frustrations may not stem from the business issue they brought up, but from personal challenges they are carrying into the conversation.

Imagine starting your meeting just ten minutes after your client got chewed out by their spouse for missing another important milestone for the kids. Their frustration might seem like it's about the delay in processing plant samples, but the root issue is the time they are missing with their family.

At moments like this, your role is to listen and respond with empathy. Instead of diving straight into business, you might ask if it would be helpful for them to wrap up early so they can get back to their family. That small moment of understanding, the sparkle in their eye or the slight smile on their face, shows you have connected with them on a deeper level. And that connection is what turns clients into raving fans.

As salespeople, our job is to truly step into the customer's world and leave our own troubles behind. We do this by asking thought-provoking questions and letting go of our own expectations about what the outcome should be. But how do we actually make this happen?

I had spent so much time learning what made our products great but not enough time learning what actually mattered to my customers. Once I stopped talking and started truly listening, everything shifted. My customers were willing to teach me, not just about their technical needs, but about the real challenges they faced every day. That is when I started to see how our solutions actually fit into their world.

If you have never taken the time to survey your existing customers and analyze their experiences, now is the time to change that. The process below will help you uncover insights that will take your conversations with prospects to a whole new level.

Stepping Into Your Customer's World

Step 1: Run a Report and Identify Accounts

Start by opening your CRM and pulling a list of all existing customers in your territory. Sort it by total revenue, highest to lowest. Make sure you include historical data, even from before you took over the territory. If your company doesn't have a CRM system, ask the accounting team to pull the numbers. You need to know who has bought, who has paused, and where the gaps are.

When I did this, I found three accounts that hadn't placed an order in nearly two years. One of them turned into my biggest deal that quarter, all because I took the time to look and reach out.

Step 2: Choose Your Growth Accounts

Now narrow your focus and choose just six accounts. Pick two from the top of the list, two from the middle, and two from the bottom. You are looking for potential—accounts that could double or even triple their spend if the right conversation happens.

Do not just choose the biggest names or the ones that talk to you the most. Look for the quiet ones. The ones with signs of life but untapped opportunity. I once picked a mid-range account that barely engaged with us. When I finally sat down with them, I discovered they had been buying from a competitor for years simply because no one asked the right question. That one conversation opened up a brand-new revenue stream.

Skip the ones where you already have 70 percent or more of their business. You are managing those, not growing them.

Step 3: Schedule Meaningful Meetings

This is the time to reconnect. Pick up the phone and reach out to the contact for each of those six accounts. Let them know you want to meet to check in, see how things are going, and understand how the product is working for them. Keep it simple, keep it clear. This is not about pitching. It is about learning.

Whenever possible, schedule virtual meetings so you can see their face and record the conversation. Those recordings are gold. You will hear things differently on the replay. If virtual is not an option, go in person. Avoid phone calls. You need to read their body language and build trust.

I once reviewed a recorded meeting where I realized I missed a critical buying signal. I followed up the next day, and it turned into a deal three times bigger than what I had expected. That would have never happened if I had just gone off memory.

Pro Tip: Make it clear this meeting is about understanding their experience, not about pitching anything new. This will set the right tone and help them feel comfortable opening up.

Step 4: Ask Targeted Questions

During the meeting, make sure you don't ask more than four questions. This keeps the conversation focused and prevents it from feeling like an interrogation. And remember, if the client takes the conversation in a direction you didn't expect, follow their lead. You can always circle back to your next question later.

Here Are Some Questions to Get You Started:

- Can you describe the challenges you were experiencing before purchasing your first product from us?
- How did those challenges impact your team or organization?
- Before deciding to work with us, what other options did you explore?
- Since implementing our product, what changes have you noticed, both positive and negative?
- What process improvements have you experienced?
- Has there been a return on your investment? If so, can you estimate how much?
- What makes you continue purchasing from us?
- Is there anything I missed or anything else you'd like to share?

If you're like me and have a bit of a scientist's brain, you'll want to keep your questions consistent across all six accounts. This helps you spot trends and identify patterns in the responses, which is what we're after here.

Pro Tip: Stick to four questions per meeting and let the client do most of the talking. This is where you uncover the gold.

Step 5: Organize and Analyze Insights

Once you've completed all six interviews, it's time to analyze your findings. Review the responses and group them into categories. Look for trends or recurring themes in the challenges, benefits, and suggestions shared by your clients.

Your finished product might look different from someone else's, and that's okay. The goal is to learn from your customers, step into their world, and start speaking their language.

Next Steps: Use these insights to tailor your conversations with prospects and create more meaningful connections.

When you follow these steps, you're not just learning about your customers; you're positioning yourself as someone who truly cares about their needs. And when you approach your prospects armed with this deeper understanding, you'll see the difference it makes in your sales conversations.

For those of you who like a bit of structure, you can find a template in your toolkit to drop your insights in.

Guess what we have just done? We stepped into our customers' world and learned how to get more customers like them.

We will use this table again, so be sure to keep it handy. For now, give yourself a clap and a high five. You have taken the first step toward becoming a customer-centric, problem-focused salesperson.

Remember, it only gets better. But let me tell you, growth is never a straight path. Before it gets better, you might stumble a little.

You hear those voices saying you don't belong and you're not good enough? We all hear them. But we don't have to listen.

In the next chapter, we are going to face those beliefs together. We will break them down and rewrite the story you tell yourself so you can step into the sales professional you are meant to be. Let's tackle this head-on. See you in the next chapter.

BELIEF Selling™ in Action: Redefining How You Sell

B | Break Barriers

- Most onboarding programs focus heavily on product training but leave out the essential sales skills
- Break free from the limiting belief that "features sell themselves" and focus on what your clients truly care about: their challenges and needs.

E | Embrace Growth

- Shift your focus from your product to your client's world.
- Stop relying on feature-dumping and embrace curiosity and empathy to build deeper connections.

L | Learn Skills

- Use the customer interview exercise to uncover insights directly from your clients.
- Analyze their feedback, identify trends, and learn how to tailor your approach to align with their priorities.

I | Implement Boldly

- Reach out to clients, ask meaningful questions, and actively listen to their responses.
- Even if this approach feels unfamiliar at first, trust the process. It leads to better results and stronger relationships.

E | Execute Consistently

- Make this process a regular part of your routine.
- Running reports, scheduling meetings, asking targeted questions, and analyzing insights consistently will sharpen your skills and help you build a customer-focused strategy.

F | Fuel Others
- Share what you learn with your team to multiply the impact.
- When you share insights and trends, you empower others and help create a culture of collaboration and success.

CHAPTER 3

Winning Starts in Your Mind

Before I turned 30, I was making well over six figures a year. Quarter after quarter, I crushed my sales targets. Year after year, I took home awards for exceeding my quota.

On paper, my life looked incredible.

I had financial security and zero debt. My kids were in top-tier private schools. We took luxurious weeklong vacations. I wore designer shoes, drove a luxury SUV, and never had to check the price tag. From the outside looking in, I had it all.

But something felt off.

After the meetings ended, after the house got quiet, and after the boys went to bed, I would sit in the stillness, surrounded by all the things I had worked so hard to earn, and feel completely disconnected.

There were nights I stared at the ceiling, wondering why I still felt empty. I had checked every box. I had followed every rule. I had achieved what many people dream of.

But joy was fleeting, and peace was nowhere to be found.

No matter how much money I made or how many trips I took, I couldn't shake the feeling that something was missing. Success, as I had defined it, wasn't filling the void in my heart or quieting the noise in my mind.

Shortly after my 30th birthday, I sought professional help for the first time in my life. That in itself was a massive step. There is a stigma around therapy, especially in high-performance careers like sales, and an even bigger stigma around admitting you need it.

Sales is a high-pressure, high-stress job. We face more losses than wins. If our job is to diagnose and solve our customers' problems all day, doesn't it make sense that we would need someone to help us process our own?

During one of my first sessions, my therapist asked me a question I will never forget.

"Wesleyne, are you proud of yourself?"

Proud?

The word made me pause. It felt strange. Unfitting, even. Pride, in my mind, was for people who changed the world. People who overcame something massive. I had not cured cancer. I was just doing what needed to be done.

I shifted in my seat. The silence stretched. Eventually, I shook my head.

"I don't see any reason to be proud. I went to college, graduated at the top of my class, got a good job, and hit my quota. That is the expectation. There is nothing special about that."

I believed pride was reserved for extraordinary accomplishments. I had responsibilities, people counting on me, goals to meet, and life to keep in motion. There was no space for pride. Only pressure.

The truth was, I was chasing the feeling of being enough. And no matter how much I achieved, I still had not felt it. I thought landing the next big account or earning the next title would get me there. That I would finally feel worthy. Finally feel seen. But that moment never came.

I watched people around me move faster, get promoted sooner, and receive the kind of recognition I quietly longed for. Every time they did, I questioned whether I was falling behind. On paper, I looked successful. But inside, I felt like I was running a race I could never win.

Then she looked at me and said something I will never forget.

"I've had a lot of people sit on that same couch. People who have faced the same childhood struggles you have. And they are nowhere near as successful as you."

That landed hard.

At that moment, I realized I had spent my entire career measuring my worth by what I could produce. I was so focused on performance that I had never learned how to simply be proud of who I had become.

Resilient. Determined. Steady.

That conversation cracked something open, and it led me somewhere I had never allowed myself to go before—a path of self-discovery.

I started learning how to celebrate small wins. I began to challenge the belief that I had to earn rest, joy, or pride. I started to redefine success, not by my numbers but by how I showed up.

And slowly, I gave myself permission to be proud.

Not just of what I accomplished, but of who I was becoming.

And that changed everything.

Let's take a deep dive into working through some of these areas together.

> *Redefining success in sales starts with how you define yourself.*

Redefining Success in Sales

Think about how you have measured success in your sales career. Has it always been about promotions, quotas, or awards? Or have you taken time to honor the personal growth, the resilience, and the skills you have developed along the way?

Many high achievers struggle to feel proud of their progress because they are always chasing the next milestone. But what if success meant something deeper?

Take five minutes. Write down three things you are proud of in your sales journey that have nothing to do with numbers.

- A time you helped a customer solve a real problem
- A moment you spoke up even though you were nervous
- The simple fact that you keep showing up, even when it is hard

Now ask yourself: Do you let those moments count? Do you allow yourself to feel proud of them? What if those quiet wins are actually the ones that matter most?

Uncovering the Beliefs That Shape You

Before we ever learn how to sell, we learn how to make sense of success and failure. Those beliefs are shaped early by parents, teachers, and experiences, and often follow us into adulthood.

Some beliefs empower us; others quietly hold us back.

When a deal falls through or a client ghosts you, what do you tell yourself? "I must not be good at this"? "People just do not want what I offer"?

Those thoughts are often not facts; they are stories. And you have the power to rewrite them.

Now Try This:

Write down one self-limiting belief you hold about yourself in sales. Then ask yourself: Is this an absolute truth? Or is it something you have repeated so many times that it feels true? Rewrite it into a self-empowering belief.

Examples:
- Instead of saying, "I am bad at cold calling," say "every call I make helps me improve and learn something new."
- Instead of saying, "I need to discount to close," say "my value is worth full price and I can communicate that clearly."

The next time the old belief shows up, replace it with the new one. Speak it until you believe it.

The Shift

Sales is not just about winning deals. It is about the relationships you build, the value you provide, and the personal growth you experience along the way.

Start recognizing all of your wins, not just the ones tied to revenue.

The Roots of Self-Worth and Its Impact on Sales

As humans, our self-worth is shaped long before we ever step into a sales role.

For most people, this begins in childhood, around the age of five. This is when we start school, navigate friendships, and begin to understand what it feels like to be included or excluded.

When we are invited to play with Barbies or LEGOs, we feel a sense of belonging. When we are left out, we experience rejection.

But the real foundation of our self-worth is built at home.

When we share our experiences with our parents, their response shapes how we process acceptance and rejection. If they dismiss our feelings, we learn to suppress them and tell ourselves that no one really cares if we always play alone, so we withdraw.

On the other hand, if our parents listen, validate our emotions, and help us come up with solutions—whether that means joining the group, finding another one, or creating our own—we learn resilience. We develop the ability to get back up after we fall.

This pattern continues throughout our lives. The way we respond to success and failure is deeply rooted in the belief systems we develop early on.

Some of these beliefs empower us, while others limit us.

A self-limiting belief is a deeply ingrained thought that holds us back, whether in selling, leading, loving, or simply living fully. These are the lies that keep us stuck and prevent us from taking the next step.

Meanwhile, a self-powering belief is the mindset shift that helps us push past those limitations. It allows us to challenge negative thoughts, reframe our experiences, and grow.

In sales, certain self-limiting beliefs are particularly common. They create invisible barriers that keep us from reaching our full potential.

Reflection Prompt

We all have beliefs that hold us back. Some are so deeply ingrained that we do not even think to question them.

When a client ghosts us after weeks of back-and-forth, what do we tell ourselves?

Maybe I am just not a natural salesperson.

Maybe cold calling is not for me.

Maybe I have to offer a discount if I want to win the business.

Where do these beliefs come from?

Did someone tell you that?

Did you fail once and decide it was true forever?

Or did you carry someone else's fear and mistake it for fact?

The stories we tell ourselves shape how we show up.

And if we do not challenge them, they become the ceiling we cannot break through.

Exercise

Write down one self-limiting belief you have about yourself in sales.

Now, challenge it. Is it an absolute fact, or is it just a story you have repeated so many times that it feels true?

Rewrite it as a self-powering belief. Here are some examples:

Instead of saying that I am bad at cold calling, say, "Every call I make is an opportunity to refine my approach and learn something new."

Instead of saying I have to offer a discount to close the deal, say, "Customers buy based on value, not price, and it is my job to communicate that value effectively."

Every time the limiting belief pops up in your mind, replace it with the new one.

> *The stories we carry shape how we show up and what we believe we are capable of.*

Rejection vs. Resilience

I do not know anyone who likes to be rejected. Not a single one.

Every person on this planet craves acceptance, but some of us take that need too far. We fear rejection so strongly that we let our prospects walk all over us.

They ask for a discount, and we cave because we think they will say no without it.

They cancel on us at the last minute, even after we flew in just to meet with them. Instead of holding our ground, we extend our trip, reschedule, and get canceled again. Because the customer is the boss, right? And we have to do whatever they say.

We send ten cold emails, get one response from someone yelling "NOT INTERESTED" in all caps, and immediately stop sending emails. We assume we are annoying everyone instead of realizing that one response does not define the other nine.

Sales is a game of losses. You will always lose more than you win. You will never bat 100, and if you do, you are playing it way too safe. Not everyone should welcome you with open arms.

So how do you overcome rejection? By shifting your focus. Stop making rejection about them and start making it about your process.

When a prospect cancels at the last minute, ask yourself what you could have done differently. Did they have a clear agenda for the meeting? Were they even a well-qualified lead in the first place? What can you change next time?

And when someone does say yes, show up on time and even extend your meeting. Afterwards, study what went right. What did you do that made them want to engage with you? What worked in your approach?

Rejection is a guarantee in sales, but taking it as an affront to your person is a choice. You will never fully understand why people do what they do, so stop obsessing over their actions. Instead, focus on yours. That is where your power is.

Reflection Prompt

Think about the last time a prospect rejected you.

How did you react? Did you take it personally? Did it discourage you?

Did you analyze what happened, or did you just move on without learning from it?

Exercise

Write down the last three times you were rejected by a prospect.

For each rejection, answer these questions:

What was the reason they said no?

What, if anything, could you have done differently?

What did you learn from the experience?

Now, rewrite the rejection as a lesson instead of a loss. Example:

Rejection: A prospect canceled the meeting at the last minute.

Lesson: I should have confirmed the agenda and commitment upfront to avoid flakiness.

The Shift

Rejection is not failure. The only failure is not learning from it.

Being Liked Won't Close Deals

As human beings, we all desire to be liked. But if our need for approval drives how we sell, we will never win business.

Think about that one cousin who is always selling something. You know the one. They are deep into the latest multi-level marketing craze, and every time they ask to come over and hang out, you already know what's coming.

They show up at your house, all smiles, and say, "This is the real deal—the absolute best supplement to reverse aging."

You humor them, letting them go through their entire presentation. They talk endlessly about how amazing the product is and how it will change your life.

I hope you are rolling your eyes right now because you can picture that cousin perfectly. You know exactly how this conversation goes every single time. And just like that, you realize they are making the same mistake that so many salespeople make.

They wrap up their pitch and hit you with, "So do you want to grab a starter pack?"

You smile, politely say no thanks, and shift the conversation to that upcoming wedding you are both dreading.

Here is the thing. You like your cousin. In fact, you love your cousin. But they brought zero value to the conversation. They never asked a single question. They never tried to understand your world. They just assumed that because you have a relationship, you would buy.

This is the same mistake salespeople make when they prioritize being liked over delivering value.

Your job is not to be everyone's friend. You already have friends and family who like you. Your prospects and customers do not need to fall into that category.

Focus on bringing value. Step into their world. Solve their problems. That is what earns trust and drives sales.

Reflection Prompt

We all want to be liked, but in sales, that desire can become a trap.

Have you ever avoided asking tough questions because you wanted to keep the conversation "comfortable"?

Have you ever given a discount without a fight just to keep the deal moving?

Have you let a prospect reschedule on you repeatedly because you were afraid to push back?

If so, you are not alone. But here is the truth: being liked will not close deals.

Exercise

Think of a time when you prioritized being liked over making the right sales decision. Maybe you gave in too easily to a discount request, let a customer waste your time, or held back from challenging their assumptions.

Now, write down how you should have handled it differently. What would you do if you were operating from confidence instead of the need for approval?

The next time you catch yourself doing this, pause and ask yourself: Am I making this decision because it is best for the sale, or because I want them to like me?

> ***Own your schedule, own your success.***

The Shift

Sales is about respect, not approval. When you lead with value, the right prospects will trust you, and trust will always close more deals than likability.

Own Your Schedule, Own Your Success

How we spend our time determines much of our success.

A poor salesperson is reactive. When a prospect sends an inquiry, they respond. When an existing client asks for a quote, they send it. When their boss tells them to make ten calls each week, they make exactly ten calls.

They do just enough to keep their job. Their success looks like staying under the radar and landing between 85 and 95 percent of their quota each year.

A great salesperson is proactive. They follow up consistently. They spend at least three days a week in the field meeting with customers. Their boss never has to tell them to make ten calls a week because they are already making twenty-five.

Their success looks like shattering their quota every single month. They finish the year at least ten percent above their goal, if not more.

So what is the difference between the two?

Strong salespeople take control of their time. They do not let the tactical parts of their job get pushed to the side. They know when they are mentally sharp and when they are sluggish.

These ninja salespeople have a dedicated power hour each day. During that power hour, they focus on the task they like the least, not the one they enjoy the most.

When I was in field sales, once I had a steady flow of business, prospecting took a backseat. I am a morning person, happily part of the 4:30 a.m. club. So, before I even checked my email, I logged into our CRM or hopped on LinkedIn to engage with brand-new people.

Before, I would wait until three p.m., scrolling and trying to connect with prospects while distracted. Instead, I started knocking it out first thing in the morning. What I did not expect was how accomplished I would feel after getting it done.

The result?

I wasn't scrambling at the end of the month, trying to drum up new business.

I actually enjoyed the process more because I was doing it when my brain was sharp.

I felt accomplished before my day even really started.

You will experience the same sense of achievement when you dedicate just one hour a day to tackling the tasks that usually trip you up.

Reflection Prompt

Think about your daily sales routine.

Do you feel like your day controls you, instead of you controlling it?

Are you constantly playing catch-up, scrambling to get things done?

Do you find yourself pushing certain tasks to "later," but later never comes?

One of the biggest differences between top performers and average salespeople is how they use their power hour—the time of day when they are mentally at their sharpest.

Are you in the five a.m. club, ready to conquer the world by eight a.m.?

Do you hit your stride in the mid-morning after your first few cups of coffee?

Do you come alive after lunch, knocking out your top priorities in record time?

Your power hour is when your brain is firing on all cylinders. And this is when you should be tackling the task you dread the most, not the one you enjoy the most.

Exercise

Identify the task you avoid the most. Be honest. No one will see this but you.

Is it cold calling?

Is it updating your CRM?

Is it following up with prospects?

Is it something else you keep "running out of time" to do?

Open your calendar and schedule a recurring one-hour appointment with yourself at the time when you are most energized. Name it exactly as it is: "Prospecting," "CRM Updates," "Follow-Ups," "Cold Calls."

Commit to this for 21 workdays (four weeks and one day). Research shows it takes 21 days to make a habit stick, whether good or bad.

Hold yourself accountable. If you try to skip your power hour, ask yourself:

Would I cancel a meeting with my boss?

Would I cancel a meeting with my most important customer?

If the answer is no, then don't cancel the most important meeting you have, your power hour.

When you dedicate just one hour a day to tackling your most dreaded tasks, you take back control of your time.

Instead of carrying the weight of that task around all day, you knock it out first and free up mental space to focus on everything else. You will experience a dopamine hit every time you complete your power hour, reinforcing the habit and making it easier to stick with.

This is how the best salespeople own their schedule.

Now it is your turn. Open your calendar and schedule your power hour right now.

Self-limiting beliefs have held all of us back at different points in our sales careers. Today, you might feel like you have everything under control, and if that is the case, kudos to you for doing the work.

But if every single word I just wrote describes you perfectly, do not let it weigh you down. Now you know why you feel overwhelmed or always rushed. You have identified what is holding you back, and that awareness is the first step.

The next step is to catch yourself before you fall into those traps. Recognize them early, shift your habits, and slowly work your way out before you get stuck.

Your beliefs dictate your actions, and your actions determine your results. Shift your mindset, take control, and watch your success transform.

As we discussed, the way we think shapes the actions we take, especially in sales. If we're not careful, we can slip into habits that restrict us, like random acts of selling. Just like poor habits start with the wrong mindset, ineffective sales practices often begin with a lack of structure and intentionality.

Now, if you're ready to stop "winging it" and start seeing real results, it's time to shift your mindset and embrace a process. A clear, repeatable sales process can transform the way you work, just as a shift in mindset can change the way you approach challenges.

In the next chapter, we'll dive into the sales process and explore how having a structured path can make all the difference in achieving your goals.

> *Change your thinking, change your sales.*

BELIEF Selling™ in Action: Change Your Thinking, Change Your Sales

B | Break Barriers

- Recognize the self-limiting beliefs that hold you back, such as tying your worth to quotas, fearing rejection, or prioritizing being liked over delivering value.
- Challenge the idea that success is only measured by external validation. Internal growth, resilience, and effort matter just as much.

E | Embrace Growth

- Replace negative self-talk with self-powering beliefs. Instead of saying, "I am bad at cold calling," reframe it as, "Every call is an opportunity to refine my approach."
- Stop focusing on why a prospect said no and start focusing on what you can learn from it. Rejection is not personal; it is part of the process.

L | Learn Skills

- Study your wins just as much as your losses. What worked? What can you repeat?
- Take ownership of your time by identifying your most productive hours. Then, use them for high-impact activities, instead of letting distractions dictate your day.

I | Implement Boldly

- Schedule a Power Hour daily to tackle the tasks you avoid the most, whether it is prospecting, follow-ups, or CRM updates.
- Push back when needed. Stop giving in to discounts or endless reschedules just because you want to be liked.

E | Execute Consistently

- Make small, intentional shifts in your mindset and daily habits. Sales success is built through repeated effort, not occasional big wins.
- Commit to consistently applying these principles for 21 days to form new habits that stick.

F | Fuel Others

- Share what you have learned with colleagues, mentees, or your team. Growth multiplies when you help others overcome the same barriers you have conquered.
- Encourage a culture where sales is about value and problem-solving, not just transactions and quotas.

CHAPTER 4

From Chaos to Consistency

As you can probably tell, I stumbled my way into sales. No formal training. No clue what I was doing. Just trying to figure things out as I went.

I fell into what I now call random acts of selling. A prospect would request a quote, and I'd send it over without ever talking to them. Then I'd follow up endlessly with "just checking in" emails.

If someone asked for an onsite demo, I'd rush to set it up and run all their samples for free without even qualifying if they were serious.

If I finally got a yes, but only if I gave them a discount, I'd immediately go to my boss. When they said no, I'd just tell the prospect, "Sorry, we can't do that."

It was a hot, horrible disaster.

But the worst part? I didn't even know how to fix it. No one, and I mean no one, took the time to teach me that there was an actual process I was supposed to follow.

After losing yet another deal, I opened my CRM and saw these words: Qualification. Discovery. Negotiation. Close. And then I paused and thought, "Wait, is this a roadmap?"

I felt like I'd discovered a hidden treasure map, but I had no idea how to read it. I realized that these words weren't just buzzwords—

they were the sales process. But how was I supposed to move a deal from one stage to the next?

By now, you have probably figured out I'm scrappy. So, I didn't just learn what each of those words meant. I built my own process, one that I still use today.

Before we get into the specifics, let's start with the foundation. The traditional sales process is shaped like a funnel because we should always have more activity at the top than at the bottom.

> *There's a process, and once you master it, everything changes.*

Your company might have a complex multi-step process, and that's okay. Work within those bounds but use this simple structure to make sure you're moving people through the pipeline.

We'll break it all down in the next chapters. For now, just know this: Selling isn't about winging it. There's a process, and once you master it, everything changes.

Finally, a Sales Process That Makes Sense

In the identity stage, this is where your leads start coming in, and they fall into two categories: marketing qualified leads (MQLs) and sales qualified leads (SQLs). Both fit the demographics of your ideal client, but the key difference is their intent to buy.

An MQL is someone who has shown passive interest but is not ready for a sales conversation yet. They might have downloaded a resource, engaged with your content, or stopped by your booth at an event. They are still gathering information. Still exploring. Still deciding if their problem is big enough to solve right now.

This becomes an SQL when they signal they are ready to engage in a real conversation. That signal could be as simple as filling out a contact form, responding to an outreach email, or saying yes to a meeting request.

Let me give you an example:

A prospect downloaded one of our white papers and liked two of my LinkedIn posts. That told me they were interested but not ready. I did not call them right away. Instead, I sent a short message thanking them for engaging with our content and shared another resource that was relevant to their industry.

Three weeks later, they replied with, "We've been discussing a project that might be a fit for your solution. Can we set up a time to talk?"

That was the moment they became an SQL.

You do not chase an MQL. You stay visible and valuable until they are ready to step forward.

However, just because they've taken a meeting doesn't mean they're fully qualified. That's your job to determine in the first conversation. To truly qualify them, you need to answer three key questions:

- Do they have a problem you can solve?
- Do they want to solve it?
- Are they willing to let you help them to fix it?

This isn't about budget, contracts, or readiness to execute immediately. It's about understanding their challenges and how committed they are to solving them.

If you can confidently answer yes to all three, congratulations; you now have a real prospect. That's when you move from the identity stage to the nurture stage.

In the nurture stage, your role shifts from being a seller to being a guide. This is where deeper discovery begins. You are not just checking boxes or reciting questions from a script. You are getting to the heart of the problem. It's time to ask: What is not working? Why does it matter right now? What happens if they do nothing?

You start uncovering what is at stake. When you do that, you shift the conversation from product to impact.

This is also where you begin to bring the right people into the conversation. That junior contact who downloaded the white paper might be your starting point, but they are not the one who controls the budget or signs the contract. Ask who else needs to be involved. Get clear on what matters to them. Listen for disconnects between departments. The earlier you understand the internal dynamics, the easier it becomes to align your solution with their goals.

And then there is the money. You are not just asking for a number. You are learning how they make investment decisions. Is this a line item they planned for? Are they reallocating funds? Do they need to build a business case to get approval?

Budget, need, authority, and timing matter, but they are not what we use to qualify or disqualify someone. They are what we pay attention to throughout the sales process to assess whether we can actually close the deal.

In one of my early opportunities, I spent three meetings with someone I thought was the decision-maker. They were not. By the time I figured it out, the window had closed. That deal taught me everything I needed to know about the importance of real discovery.

The discovery stage is not about pushing. It is about guiding with intention.

You are creating clarity. You are building alignment. And you are making it easier for the buyer to say yes because you took the time to understand their world first.

Once you fully understand their pain points, their problems, and their impact on their organization, you decide if a demo is necessary to move things forward.

If you do a demo, focus on no more than five features. Every single one should be directly tied to the challenges you uncovered during discovery.

Most deals are lost by overcomplicating the demo. We get excited to show off all the cool features and capabilities, but that makes the demo about the product, not the customer. A customer-centric demo focuses only on the specific challenges your prospect needs to solve, not on overwhelming them with features they may never use.

For example, you might say, "You mentioned that defects aren't being caught until final assembly. This inline camera can be programmed to detect defects as soon as they happen."

Think about your phone. How many features have you never touched? Take the measuring tape app. I've had this brand of phone for 13 years and used that app maybe three times. If a salesperson had tried to sell me on that feature along with 50 others I didn't need, I would have walked away.

Drill this into your brain. A maximum of five features in your demo. *Period.*

Whether you do a demo or not, the next step is presenting the proposal. No more emailing quotes and hoping for the best. You present it in a way that connects their problems to your solution.

Always schedule a proposal review meeting to walk them through what you've put together. In that meeting, listen for the micro-yes and ask for the order verbally.

Asking for the order out loud allows you to handle objections in real time and make sure you're aligned before sending over the final quote or proposal.

If you don't follow a structured sales process, your close rates will be dismal, and your conversion rates will suffer. As a result, you'll stay stuck in random acts of selling.

The Math Behind a Full Funnel

We've already established that the sales process is a funnel, not a straight line. But why does that matter so much?

Simple. It matters because you will always need more leads entering the process than deals closing at the end. If you are only focused on what is closing, you are missing the bigger picture. A healthy funnel starts at the top.

One of the questions I get asked most often is, "How many leads do I actually need?"

The answer depends on your conversion rates.

Let me give you a real example.

I once worked with a rep named Marcus who had a monthly goal of closing five new deals. He felt like he was doing everything he could. His days were packed with meetings and follow-ups, yet his results were inconsistent.

When we looked at his numbers, we saw that he was converting about 33 percent at each stage of his funnel. That meant for every three leads he qualified, only one was moving forward.

So we worked backward from his goal.

He wanted to close five deals. To do that, he needed 15 proposals. To get those 15 proposals, he needed 45 nurtured prospects. And to reach 45 nurtures, he needed 139 qualified leads at the top of his funnel.

That was the turning point. He realized the issue wasn't his follow-up or his close rate. He just wasn't bringing in enough at the top. Once he saw the full picture, he stopped chasing the wrong numbers. His outreach became more focused. His energy shifted. Within two months, he was not only hitting his goal but doing it with less stress.

For math nerds like me, you can use this equation: Total Leads Needed = Closed Deals ÷ (Conversion Rate ^ Number of Stages)

For this example:

Total Leads Needed = 5 ÷ (0.33 ^ 3) = 139

If formulas are not your thing, keep it simple.

Think in **threes.**
For every deal you want to close, you need
Three Proposals
Nine Nurtures
Twenty-Seven Leads

So for five deals, that's 15 proposals, 45 nurtures, and between 135 and 140 leads.

This is not about being perfect with math. It is about being clear with your process. When you know your numbers, you stop guessing and start leading yourself toward consistent success.

If your conversion rates at each stage are higher, you'll need fewer leads at the top. If they're lower, you'll need more. This is why tracking your numbers is so critical. When you know your own conversion rates, you can set realistic targets and make sure you're consistently filling your funnel with the right number of leads.

The biggest mistake salespeople make is not having enough activity at the top of the funnel. If you aren't consistently bringing in new leads, you'll never have enough opportunities to close at the bottom. Sales is all about volume, strategy, and consistency. When you understand the numbers, you take control of your results.

Fixing Your Wonky Funnel

After going through the exercise of analyzing your pipeline and conversion rates, you might have started noticing some strange trends. Some stages have high conversion rates, while others are shockingly low. I call these wonky funnels.

If your conversion rate is over 90 percent at every stage, you have what I call a cylinder funnel. Every lead that enters is almost guaranteed to close. Before you pat yourself on the back, this is not a good thing. It tells me you are playing it safe. You are either only going after business that is well within your comfort zone, or you are not entering all your leads into the CRM.

The fix is to push yourself. Set a goal to add 20 percent more leads this month than last month. If you are holding back on entering leads into the CRM, stop. Make it a habit to track every new lead you identify or are assigned.

Maybe you focus on two or three big deals at a time, betting they will carry you to your quota each quarter. You take pride in playing the long game. But every three months, you find yourself scrambling to make up for lost time. By year-end, you're sitting at 95 percent of your goal, wondering what went wrong.

I coached a rep named Sean who worked this exact way. He built his quarter around two large opportunities. One moved forward. The other stalled, then disappeared. Without additional deals in his pipeline, he had no way to recover. It was not a lack of skill or effort. It was a lack of consistent deal flow.

Big deals have a place, but they should not be your entire strategy. Long-term plays only work when supported by short-term movement. A healthy pipeline includes a mix of deal sizes so that progress is steady, not sporadic.

The long game is risky. Your funnel ends up inverted, which means you are constantly teetering between success and disaster. This year, you might hit quota, but next year, you could find yourself at 60 percent. When you put all your eggs in one basket, external factors you cannot control—like budget cuts, economic shifts, or a competitor slashing prices—can wipe out six months of work in an instant.

To be successful, you need a diverse book of business. If you have a few large accounts, start looking at different departments or locations to drum up new opportunities. If you are only calling on the top 20 percent of your accounts, you are leaving money on the table. Expand your reach and engage with brand-new prospects.

Now, for those of you who are great at filling the top of the funnel but struggle to move deals through, your issue is a bloated funnel. Deals flow in, you qualify them, and then they just sit in the nurture stage forever.

You take prospects to lunch, then a fishing trip, and then you present the proposal to the selection committee. Finally, there is the golf tournament. All the while, you have never once asked for the sale.

You nurture so much that your deals get stuck in the middle. Your pipeline looks healthy because it is packed with opportunities, but your pipeline velocity, which is the rate at which deals move through the process, is terrible. As a result, your close rate suffers.

> *Fixing your wonky funnel is the first step toward predictable revenue.*

If this sounds like you, it is time to start asking for the sale. Stop over-nurturing and start closing.

At this point, you have a solid understanding of the sales process. You know how to move deals from stage to stage, what conversion metrics to target, and where things can go wrong.

A repeatable sales process is the key to long-term success. You cannot improve what you do not measure. Track everything. When problems arise, your data will show you exactly where to focus so you can fix it fast.

Now that we've discussed how to build a repeatable and effective sales process, it's time to look beyond your own strategy and understand the competitive landscape.

In the next chapter, we'll dive into competitive analysis and SWOT, two powerful tools that will help you gain insights into your competitors and your own business. By evaluating your strengths, weaknesses, opportunities, and threats, you'll be able to position yourself strategically and refine your sales process to stay ahead in the game.

BELIEF Selling™ in Action: Mastering the Sales Process

B | Break Barriers

- Recognize when you're falling into random acts of selling and challenge yourself to build a clear, repeatable process.
- Break the cycle of winging it by understanding the stages of your sales process—Identify, Nurture, Demo, Proposal, Close.

E | Embrace Growth

- Understand that a structured process gives you control over your sales results. It's not about luck or chance; it's about strategy.
- Shifting from disorganization to a clear process will empower you to handle leads more effectively and efficiently.

L | Learn Skills

- Track your conversion rates at each stage of the sales process to identify what's working and what's not.
- Use your data to set realistic goals for the number of leads you need at the top of the funnel to hit your target at the bottom.

I | Implement Boldly

- Apply the process by adding more leads, diversifying your book of business, and refining your approach to asking for the sale.
- Push yourself to enter every lead into your CRM and focus on taking action rather than just nurturing opportunities forever.

E | Execute Consistently

- Keep your funnel full by consistently bringing in new leads and tracking your pipeline.
- Make sure to move deals through the process with a clear intent to qualify, nurture, and close, rather than letting them stall in the middle.

F | Fuel Others

- As you refine your process, share your insights and strategies with others on your team to help them improve their results.
- By fostering a culture of measurement and continuous improvement, you inspire others to follow the process and achieve success.

By following the BELIEF framework, you're not just implementing a sales process. You're building a habit of success that will guide you through every stage of the funnel. Track your progress, adjust when needed, and watch your results improve.

CHAPTER 5

Building Your Competitive Edge

At a tradeshow in Corpus Christi, TX, my number one competitor approached me. I smiled, stretched out my hand, and introduced myself.

He didn't shake it. Instead, he looked me straight in the eye and said, "I already know who you are. You've been stealing a lot of my customers."

My stomach dropped for a second. I wasn't sure if he was about to start an argument or make a scene. But something quickly shifted. I felt a wave of pride rise up in me, not because I was trying to take anything, but because my work was being noticed. My impact was undeniable. My name was being talked about in rooms I hadn't walked into yet.

I smiled even wider.

A few weeks earlier, I had seen his name pop up in my LinkedIn notifications. He had been watching. Studying. Trying to figure out what I was doing differently. That told me everything I needed to know.

It takes a certain skill to capture the attention of prospects your competitor is ignoring. But it takes even more to turn that attention into action.

To truly succeed in a competitive market, you need to understand your competition better than they understand themselves. It is not enough to say your product is the best. You need to know exactly why it is better, what it outperforms, and how it solves the problems they are too distracted to notice.

I recently went through something similar when I was in the market for a new car. My last car, a Mazda CX-9, had served me well for seven years. It never gave me major electrical or mechanical issues. I only had to change the oil, replace the tires, and swap out the battery twice. The long-term cost of ownership was fantastic.

When I started thinking about upgrading, my heart was set on getting another Mazda, but I decided to keep an open mind. I visited dealerships for Toyota, Honda, and Nissan, but most of what I saw didn't impress me. That is until I came across the Toyota Crown.

Keep in mind, my point of reference was my seven-year-old Mazda. So, all my questions were about how these new cars compared to my old one. The salesperson who ultimately sold me the Crown didn't bash Mazda or tell me why Toyota was far superior. Instead, he listened carefully to what I liked about my Mazda and showed me how the Crown could take those same features and elevate them.

For instance, he talked about the smooth ride and the quiet interior, but what really caught my attention was how, even though the Crown was a sedan, its 20-inch wheels gave it a higher stance, much like an SUV. That was exactly the kind of upgrade I was looking for.

What really stood out to me, though, was how well he knew both his product and his competition. He didn't need to tear down Mazda or any other car in its class. Instead, he highlighted the strengths of the Crown in ways that resonated with me, showcasing where it excelled without the need for comparison.

The key takeaway here is that to win customers, you need to know your own product inside and out, but you also need to understand your competition just as well.

You may find yourself returning to this chapter often, and that is exactly what it is here for. Before you can sell with confidence, you need a clear understanding of where your company stands. That starts with a SWOT analysis, which helps you assess your strengths, weaknesses, opportunities, and threats. We will walk through how to build a clear and honest SWOT profile so you can lean into what sets you apart and take action where growth is needed.

Once we have your SWOT in place, we'll dive into a competitive analysis of your top two competitors. This is where you'll learn how to size up what they're doing well and where they might be missing the mark. It's not about bad-mouthing the competition; it's about knowing them so well that you can confidently highlight where you have the edge.

Just like when I was looking for a new car and knew what I liked about my Mazda, you'll learn how to recognize the strengths of your product and the gaps in what your competitors offer. With this knowledge, you'll be able to make better decisions and position yourself in a way that really speaks to your customers' needs.

Let's dive in!

Building a SWOT for Growth

A SWOT analysis (strengths, weaknesses, opportunities, and threats) helps you take a deep look at your company. Each section has a purpose and gives you valuable insights. We'll break it into two parts: internal and external. Strengths and weaknesses are internal, while opportunities and threats are external factors.

Let's start with strengths. These are the things your company consistently does well. The qualities your customers feel but may never fully articulate. The value you bring makes someone choose you and stay with you.

Strength is not always loud. Sometimes it shows up quietly. Maybe you are known for fast responses. Maybe your process feels smoother than anyone else's. Maybe your team has deep industry knowledge that helps customers solve problems they could not solve on their own.

For me, one of our biggest strengths was technical support. I did not fully realize it until a customer told me, "No one else follows up the way you do. I don't have to chase you. You always show up with answers."

That shifted my perspective. I started paying closer attention to what customers praised, not just what I thought mattered. Over time, I realized that kind of support was something our competitors could not touch. It became one of my most powerful selling points.

Your strengths are not just what you do. They are what your customers remember and what they value enough to stay loyal, even if another option is cheaper.

So take your time here and write down everything. Even the things that feel small. Even the things that feel obvious. We will refine this later. Right now, your job is to name everything that makes your business work.

Now let's talk about weaknesses. This part can feel uncomfortable, but it is one of the most important steps in building a clear sales strategy. Companies rarely advertise their flaws, and it is easy to overlook the areas that need work when you are focused on what is going well.

But if we do not acknowledge what is broken, we cannot fix it.

Start by asking yourself: What do customers complain about? What do internal teams grumble about when no one is watching? Where do deals stall or fall apart?

Maybe your website is outdated or slow. Maybe it takes days to respond to support tickets. Maybe your lead times are long and your competitors can deliver faster. Sometimes the weakness is behind the scenes, like losing experienced service technicians with no clear succession plan.

I remember working with a company where everything looked polished on the outside, but under the surface, their internal communication was messy. Sales and operations clashed. Promises were made that could not be kept. It was costing them deals and damaging relationships. Naming that weakness was not easy, but once we did, we could finally start fixing it.

Be honest with yourself. If a prospect complains about their current vendor's clunky ordering system and your website is just as frustrating, do not pretend it is not a problem. Integrity in the sales process starts with knowing the full truth about what you are offering.

Aim for at least three weaknesses. If nothing comes to mind, ask someone in customer service or operations. They will tell you where the breakdowns are. And that honesty is what will help you build something stronger.

Next, look for opportunities. This section focuses on growth for your territory, not the company's overall growth, but yours. We're looking for ways you can make more money, not just ideas for the higher-ups that might never be acted on.

Think about the product lines you rarely sell. Could your existing customers use more of what you offer? What about parts of your territory you've ignored? Sure, it's not fun to drive long distances for just a few potential clients, but your competitors probably aren't eager to make those trips either.

Look at your current clients. Do you win a lot with a specific demographic? When I was in sales, my best clients were new professors outfitting their labs. They had limited budgets and cared about long-term costs, exactly what I excelled at. I made sure to stay on top of every new hire in the engineering, chemistry, and geology departments.

This section is crucial. Take your time with it. The opportunities you find here will be your roadmap for long-term growth.

Finally, let's talk about threats. These are external factors that you cannot control, but that can still impact your ability to grow and serve your customers well.

Threats might include new competitors entering your market, changing customer expectations, regulatory shifts, supply chain issues, or even negative press that shapes how people perceive your company.

Unlike weaknesses, threats do not come from inside your business. But that does not mean you are powerless. Your job is to recognize these risks early and think strategically about how to respond.

Start by asking yourself: What changes are happening in my industry that could affect sales? Are there new players offering lower prices or faster delivery? Is there new legislation that could shift how my product is used or sold?

Now take it a step further. For each threat, ask: What can I do to prepare for this? How can I turn this into a competitive edge? What specific action can I take right now to minimize the risk and position myself for success?

If a new competitor is gaining attention for their sustainability practices, maybe that is a sign to highlight your own environmental efforts more clearly. If new regulations are coming, maybe you can position your company as a trusted guide through the changes.

And here is a quick tip: If you find a threat that is within your control to fix, it is not actually a threat. It is a weakness. Move it there and make a plan to improve it.

Threats are not always bad news. Sometimes they are the push you need to sharpen your message, improve your offer, or lead the conversation in your industry.

I'll admit, I had a lot of fun writing this. I hope you enjoy completing your SWOT analysis as much as I enjoyed putting this together.

Remember, this is a living document. Review and update it twice a year, once in January to kick off the year and again in July to check your progress. If your fiscal year doesn't align with the calendar, review it at the start of your fiscal year and at the midpoint.

I live for reviewing SWOTs. Send your copy to me at reset@transformedsales.com. I promise I read every email, but I may not respond to it. To hold yourself accountable, send the SWOT over within two weeks of reading this chapter.

Competitive Edge: Analyzing Your Competition

Now that you have your SWOT, it is time to look outside of your company and into the world your buyers are navigating. This is where competitive analysis begins.

But this is not about copying what your competitors are doing or obsessing over what they have that you do not. This is about awareness. It is about understanding the landscape so you can position yourself with confidence and clarity.

In this exercise, we are not covering everything. We are only looking at two things: your competitors' strengths and weaknesses.

Forget their opportunities and threats for now. Every business faces external pressures. What truly impacts your sales is what your competitors do well and where they fall short.

You might not think you have direct competition, but you do. Sometimes your biggest competitor is the status quo. The buyer who says, "We're fine for now." The company that chooses to do nothing, not because they are satisfied, but because change feels hard.

When that moment comes and they are finally ready to move forward, the question becomes: will they choose you?

You cannot answer that if you do not understand who else is in the room.

How to Analyze Your Competitors

Start with the obvious players. Choose your top two competitors. The ones you hear about the most. The ones that come up when you lose a deal. The ones your prospects are comparing you to.

Then follow these steps.

Step 1: Study Their Positioning

Go to their "About Us" page and really read it. Look at the language.

What are they proud of?

Are they talking about speed, quality, innovation, or service?

Why this matters:

This tells you the story they are sharing with the market. When you understand how they are positioning themselves, you can find a way to position yourself more powerfully.

Your action: Write down three things they claim make them different.

Step 2: Scan for Weakness

Look at Google reviews. Check job sites for employee feedback. Look for patterns.

Are customers frustrated with delays?

Are employees talking about leadership issues or poor communication?

Why this matters: Weaknesses reveal opportunity. If they are slow to respond, talk about your responsiveness. If they are inconsistent, lead with your reliability. Gaps create space for you to step in and serve better.

Your action: Write down two areas where they are falling short and how you can meet that need more effectively.

Step 3: Watch Their Behavior

Scroll through their social media.

What kind of content are they posting?

How are people engaging?

Are their followers asking questions? Sharing? Ignoring?

Why this matters: Social media reveals more than branding. It shows how the market is responding, whether they are building community or just making noise.

Your action: Write one observation about how they show up online and how it compares to the presence you want to build.

If you've won clients from a competitor, call them. Ask what they liked and didn't like about working with that competitor. Be careful not to bash the competition. Keep it professional and let them know you're gathering info for a project.

Once you've gathered everything, you should have a solid page or two of notes. Now go through it all and toss out anything irrelevant. If an employee was fired for being late and complained about it online, that's not going to help you.

When you analyze, think of their strengths as comparative strengths and their weaknesses as comparative weaknesses—we're comparing their strengths to yours and their weaknesses to yours.

There's a table in your supplemental guide to show you exactly how this should look. Use it.

Step back and evaluate where you've been spending your energy. Are you unknowingly competing in areas where your competitors have the upper hand? If a local university's mechanical engineering department is heavily funded by a loyal donor, it may not be worth your time. Instead, focus on where your competitors fall short. If they lack an online ordering system, highlight how your seamless process makes it easy for customers to place and track orders under $5,000. Lean into your strengths where their weaknesses are clear.

This exercise is something most salespeople will skip. You could breeze through this chapter and think, "I'll get to it later," but you'll be hurting yourself if you do.

By knowing where your company shines, where it's weak, and where your competitors are vulnerable, you'll have better conversations with prospects and customers. When you learn where your competitors fall short, you'll be nearly untouchable.

Stop putting it off and get to work.

Now, it's time to take what you've learned and turn it into results. Get out there, execute, and start seeing the impact. You've got this.

By now, we've likely been on this journey together for a while, and I'm sure you're eager to get out in the field and start closing deals. I bet you're ready to start talking to prospects and making things happen.

But here's the question: who should you be talking to? Should it be the CEO, the VP of Operations, or the floor supervisor? Spending time with the wrong person is a surefire way to end up at the bottom of the leaderboard. So, let's dive into understanding your prospects' buying situation and how to figure out exactly who you should be targeting.

BELIEF Selling™ in Action: Building a Competitive Edge

You've got the knowledge and the tools. Now it's time to put them to work. Here's how to take action using the BELIEF framework:

B | Break Barriers

- Challenge the belief that you don't have competition.
- Even if it's the "do nothing" competitor, that's still competition.
- Acknowledge it, and you'll start seeing more opportunities.

E | Embrace Growth

- Stop thinking "I don't know what to do" and start thinking "I've got what it takes."
- Focus on your strengths, your knowledge, and the gaps in your competition.
- That's where your power lies.

> **When you tie your solution to a clear, undeniable impact, you're not just selling; you're solving something that matters.**

L | Learn Skills

- The market is always changing.
- Keep learning. Stay sharp.
- The more you know, the more you're able to adapt and win.

I | Implement Boldly

- Don't just sit on the sidelines.
- Go out there and use what you know.
- Execute with confidence. Bold moves lead to real results.

E | Execute Consistently

- Success is all about consistency.
- Don't let your knowledge gather dust.

- Keep applying what you've learned, refining your approach, and driving forward.

F | Fuel Others

- Share what you've learned.
- When you help others grow, it strengthens your own game.
- Teach, mentor, and lift up those around you.

CHAPTER 6

The Power of the Buying Committee

You followed the process.

The prospect was engaged. The conversation felt genuine. The solution was a good fit.

They said, "This looks great. Let me run it by my team."

And then nothing.

No updates. No feedback. No decision.

Not because your proposal missed the mark or because your pricing was too high, but because you were talking to the wrong person or just one person.

This happens more often than most salespeople realize. The meeting feels like a yes, but the outcome quietly slips into a no. In complex sales, the person you are speaking with is rarely the only one involved in the decision.

There is always another voice, another opinion, and another layer of influence.

That is why understanding buyer personas is not optional; it is essential.

When you understand who you are selling to—not just their title, but what drives them—everything shifts. You stop chasing approval and start building trust. You learn to speak to different needs. You begin to see the full decision process instead of reacting to the surface.

In every B2B sale, multiple people influence the decision. They determine what to buy, when to buy, and who to buy from.

Seventy percent of lost sales happen because salespeople either focus on the wrong person or fail to engage enough people. Deals fall apart, not because the solution was wrong, but because the salesperson never reached those who held the real power.

You will never sell to just one person. Not in this kind of sale. Not if you want to win consistently.

In every B2B sale, multiple people influence the final decision: what to buy, when to buy, and who to buy from.

Think about the last three sales you lost. How many people in that company did you actually engage with? Were there names that kept coming up, but you ignored them or assumed they weren't important?

A buying committee is a group of active or passive decision-makers involved in any purchase. The size varies, but on average, there are seven people involved. No, they don't all need to be in the same meeting, but you do need to identify and engage them.

Within every account, you'll always find three key players:

Influencers—The ones shaping opinions behind the scenes.

The Decision Maker—The one with final approval.

An Internal Champion—The person who fights for you when you're not in the room.

If you're not identifying these players early on, you're leaving your deals to chance.

Mastering the buying committee isn't optional; it's the difference between losing deals and closing them.

Influencers Have Opinions, Not Power

Let's start with the influencers. Most of the buying committee falls into this category.

Influencers are the people who interact with your product, provide feedback, and often sit in meetings where vendors are being discussed. They do not make decisions. They rarely advocate. But they always have an opinion that can sway the room.

They do not open doors. They do not go to bat for you. They will not help you navigate the organization. They will answer questions when asked, and they may even test your product, but that is the extent of their involvement.

They can be office managers, purchasing agents, plant floor workers, lab techs, or technical support staff. If they touch the product or see its impact but are not in charge of selecting or approving it, they are likely an influencer.

Back when I was a chemist working in the lab, I was an influencer. I helped evaluate equipment. I provided samples for testing. I attended sales presentations, but I did not care which vendor we chose. I just wanted something newer than the twenty-year-old system we were limping along with.

When a salesperson followed up with me, I usually responded with, "That's above my pay grade."

Sometimes I didn't respond at all.

Not because I didn't appreciate their effort, but because talking to salespeople wasn't part of my job. I had data to analyze. I had deadlines to meet. And unless they were bringing food or giving away something I wanted, their outreach was easy to ignore.

That is the truth about influencers. They often do not feel like they *owe* you a response, and they will not move your deal forward unless someone else asks for their input.

So what should you do with this?

First, learn to recognize them. Influencers give practical feedback but stay neutral. They tell you what works or what doesn't but never ask deeper questions. They do not bring others into the conversation and rarely say no, but they also won't help you get to yes.

Second, adjust your expectations. Your job is not to turn them into internal champions. It is to respect their role, gather insight, and avoid wasting energy trying to create momentum where none exists.

Third, engage them with intention. If you are going to reach out, make it worthwhile. Offer something of value by bringing lunch, asking about their workflow, or including them in a product demo so they can give input. Let them feel heard, even if they are not the ones making the final call.

And finally, do not mistake their attention for authority. Too many deals get stuck because the salesperson builds rapport with an influencer and assumes they are more powerful than they are. If they are not connecting you to others, if they are not talking about next steps, and if they keep saying "I'll pass this along," they are not your decision-maker.

Influencers are part of the buying process, but they are not *your* buyer.

Treat them with respect. Learn from them. But save your energy for the people who can say yes or no.

Chasing Decision Makers Slows You Down

As salespeople, we are always taught to go straight to the decision maker. The CEO or VP of Operations has the authority to sign contracts and approve spending, so it makes sense to target them first. This is absolutely true. The highest-ranking person in the organization can say yes or no, and that decision can make or break your deal.

But here is the reality. Executives have no time—and I mean no time—for salespeople. They know their organization has challenges, but they are not the ones solving most of them. Decision makers are critical to the buying process, but if you focus only on them, you will drag your deals out for months longer than necessary.

Unlike influencers, decision makers will open doors for you. If your message is compelling enough, they will introduce you to their right-hand person. This is the person who actually has the problem that needs solving and the time to spend with you. That introduction is a signal that you are on the right track.

Decision makers will take meetings. But do not be surprised if they reschedule at the last minute. Notice I said reschedule, not cancel. That distinction matters. Influencers cancel because your meeting is not a priority. Decision makers reschedule because their time is limited, not because they are uninterested.

Most decision makers sit in the C-suite. Sometimes it is the CEO, COO, CHRO, or CFO. Other times it is a Director or VP. The higher the price of what you are selling, the higher you need to go to get the final yes.

Let's say you sell commercial HVAC systems. If a company needs to replace one unit at a single site, the VP of Operations may be the right person. If that VP can approve purchases up to $25,000, they can sign off on that deal. But if six months later the company wants to replace fifteen units across multiple buildings, that decision is now over their approval limit. The VP is no longer your decision maker. Now, it is the CEO.

This is where many salespeople get stuck. They spend all their time trying to book meetings with executives who do not know them, trust them, or see the urgency yet. That approach slows you down.

So how do you engage decision makers without wasting time?

- Start by giving value before asking for their time. Share a short insight or pattern you are seeing in the market that connects to their priorities.
- Keep your ask small and clear. Instead of asking for a full meeting, invite them into a quick conversation to get their perspective.
- When they reschedule, follow up with patience and purpose. Reiterate why the conversation matters and offer to reconnect when it fits their calendar.
- Pay attention to how they respond. If they forward your email, copy others, or delegate a next step, they are listening.

We will get into how to build a path to the decision-maker soon. For now, keep in mind that it begins by shifting your mindset. You are not chasing people; you are opening conversations that matter.

The Unsung Hero of Every Closed Deal

Your internal champion is the person who makes or breaks the deal. They are the ones dealing with the biggest problems, challenges, and pains, and they are on a mission to solve them. It is not enough for them to be annoyed by an issue; they have to be committed to fixing it.

This is the person who will advocate for you when you are not in the room. You will educate them so thoroughly on your products and solutions that they can explain them even better than you can. An internal champion will never ignore your calls or emails. They will introduce you to key people in the organization and open multiple doors for you.

Here is the thing: your internal champion rarely has the authority to sign a contract. They usually do not control the budget either. However, they know exactly how much budget is available and who needs to be on board to get the deal across the finish line.

I call this person your raving fan.

Think about your favorite sports team or musician. How do you show your support? You buy their merchandise, attend their games or concerts, and tell everyone how amazing they are. That is exactly what your internal champion should be doing for you.

Years after I stopped selling capital equipment, my brother—who was a supervisor at a chemical company that had been one of my customers—sent me a picture of an old email I had written with instructions on how to perform a task on an instrument. He followed it up with, "My boss still talks about the great support you provided him." It had been three years since I left that role, and my internal champion was still talking about me.

As salespeople, we should all aim to build relationships with internal champions—people inside the organization who believe in our work and help us succeed from the inside.

An internal champion does not just like you; they trust you. They advocate for your solution when you are not in the room. They introduce you to decision-makers in other departments. They make time to meet when you are in town. And often, they become the reason your deal moves forward.

One of my most meaningful client relationships began with hesitation.

During our first meeting, the Director of HR asked, "What degrees do you have besides chemistry?"

"None," I answered.

"Any coaching or training certifications?"

"No."

She paused and said, "We usually work with consultants who have a stronger educational background. I'm not sure about you."

I responded with, "I understand."

The only reason I was sitting in that meeting was that someone inside the company, my internal champion, had worked with me in another region. She had seen the results for herself and believed I could do the same for this new team. That belief opened the door.

We started small: one team, one pilot.

That was four years ago.

In our most recent conversation, the same HR leader said, "Wesleyne, how do you do what you do? The results you've achieved in just six months are unlike anything I've ever seen. You helped this team recover their budget shortfall and exceed it by $10 million. You are simply incredible, and we are fortunate to work with you."

That transformation did not happen because of a sales pitch. It happened because I invested in building trust. I stayed present. I listened. I delivered results. And I stayed committed even when things were uncertain.

That is the power of an internal champion.

They are not won by charm; they are earned through consistency, credibility, and care.

If you want to create strong internal champions, here is where to start:

- Listen with intention. Understand what they are trying to achieve, not just what you are selling.
- Deliver early wins. Help them look good by making their life easier, not harder.

- Protect their influence. Never put them at risk. Keep your promises. Respect their position.
- Stay in touch. Keep showing up, even when there is no immediate deal on the table.
- Add value. Send insights, share wins, and celebrate their success too.

Internal champions are not found; they are developed.

And when you nurture those relationships well, they will carry your name further than any pitch deck ever could.

Your job as a salesperson is to make your raving fan look good. When their light shines brighter, so does yours.

Triage Your Deals: Finding the Key Players

That was a lot of information, and you might be thinking, "That's great, Wesleyne, but where do I start? How do I uncover what role each person plays in the accounts I'm calling on?"

Let's start by doing some triage.

First, pull a report of all the deals you won over the past 24 months. Take a close look at the titles of the people involved in those deals. What titles show up the most?

You should notice a trend. In about 50 to 60 percent of the deals you closed, the person you were in contact with likely had similar titles. If you don't see at least half of your deals tied to a few common titles, you're falling into the trap of random acts of selling. This means there is no clear process or strategy guiding your efforts, and we need to build some structure.

> *Triage your deals by finding the key players who truly move things forward.*

You might notice a two- or three-way tie between specific titles. If that's the case, choose one to focus on for the rest of this book.

When I find myself torn, I like to pick the titles that bring in the most revenue and are the easiest to work with.

Now, you've identified the title of your internal champion.

A few things to keep in mind about internal champions:

- Each product line you sell might have a different internal champion.
- Each industry or vertical you sell into might have a different internal champion.
- In smaller companies, the internal champion and decision maker could be the same person.

For now, I want you to focus on one product line and one industry you sell into. This should be your biggest revenue generator or the area with the most growth potential. Once you've nailed this down and have a fully baked cake, you can repeat the same exercise for your other products and industries.

Now, let's dig a little deeper.

Pull a report for the deals you have lost over the same period. Just like before, look at the titles of the people involved in those deals. Identify the titles that show up most frequently and make a note of the top three. We will come back to these in the next chapter.

Chances are, the titles from your lost deals belong to influencers, not internal champions. This is important because it highlights where your focus might have been misplaced.

At this point, you have a clearer picture of the buying committee. You know who is involved, and now you can start listening for signals that help you understand each person's role in the process. We have identified the title and the key attributes of our internal champion, but recognizing them is just the first step.

You have identified the right people, but identifying them is not enough. The next step is where the real magic happens. How do you build a deeper connection with your internal champion? How do you uncover the problems and challenges they are facing?

In the next chapter, we will dive into how to fully step into your internal champion's world by identifying the problems they are experiencing and the impact those problems have on their business.

BELIEF Selling™ in Action: Unlocking the Power of the Buying Committee

To succeed in complex sales, you need more than product knowledge. You need to understand how buying decisions are really made. The BELIEF framework will help you break down barriers, build real relationships, and close deals consistently.

B | Break Barriers

- Barrier: Thinking the decision maker is the only person who matters.
- Truth: Influencers and internal champions play huge roles in moving deals forward. Ignore them, and you're leaving money on the table.
- Barrier: Believing you need fancy degrees or certifications to succeed.
- Truth: Results speak louder than credentials. Your ability to connect with people and deliver value is what wins deals.

E | Embrace Growth

- Stop chasing titles. Build relationships with the people who actually make things happen, no matter their job description.
- Your experience and results matter more than any letters after your name. Own that.

L | Learn Skills

- Look back at your past deals. Who helped you win? Who stalled the process? Find the patterns.
- When you know how the buying committee works, you can navigate it with confidence and control.

I | Implement Boldly

- Pull reports from your last 24 months of deals—both wins and losses. See who was involved and adjust your strategy.
- Connect with internal champions. Get to the heart of their problems and show them how you can solve them.

E | Execute Consistently

- Don't just reach out once and hope for the best. Keep the conversation going at every level of the buying committee.
- Apply this approach across all your accounts and industries. Rinse and repeat.

F | Fuel Others

- Turn your internal champions into raving fans. They should be singing your praises when you're not in the room.
- Give them everything they need to confidently talk about your solutions like they're part of your sales team.

When you apply the BELIEF framework, you'll stop chasing random leads and start building real relationships. This will lead to consistent, repeatable wins.

CHAPTER 7

The Power of Impact: Turning Problems Into Opportunities

It was a hot Texas afternoon. I wish I could say I was sipping iced tea by the pool when the call came in, but the truth is, I was deep in emails, grinding through a full day. A large electronics manufacturer was in trouble. Their new product had just gone into production, and quality control was rejecting units left and right. To the naked eye, everything looked perfect. But under a microscope, micro-scratches covered the casing.

They had ruled out damage from tools or hard surfaces. After digging deeper, they suspected the coating was not bonding properly. I could hear the tension in their voices. This wasn't a small issue. They were losing time, money, and patience.

I cleared my calendar, packed a bag, and was at their Austin facility within 48 hours.

The first thing I asked for was a plant tour. Not just to check boxes. I wanted to see how they worked, meet the people on the floor, and listen. I asked about their processes, their pressure points, and what slowed them down. That is where the truth lives—in the details, in the rhythms of their day, not in the conference room slides.

Then I set up my instrument in their lab and got to work. Most competitors would have sent the samples to a central lab or shown up with polished demo samples. But I had been a chemist. I knew how to test on the spot and troubleshoot in real time.

We tested two samples. One was smooth. The other showed the same micro-streaks from earlier. Within an hour, I had the answer. At a certain production speed, the coating was losing its elasticity. It was breaking down before it could fully cover the surface.

When I explained what was happening, the room got quiet. Then came the questions. You could feel the tension shift. This was not just a technical problem anymore. It had a name. It had a cause. And it had a solution.

By the next morning, a $200,000 purchase order was in my inbox.

That moment reminded me of what sales really is. Not a pitch. Not a perfect demo. It is about showing up, diagnosing the real issue, and walking the client from stress to clarity.

Over my sales career, I have toured hundreds of facilities. If my host didn't offer a tour, I would ask to see the office, the plant, the lab, wherever the work was happening. You learn so much just by walking around and being curious. When I sold specialty chemicals, I would scan the facility for competitors' materials. If I saw a mix of brands, I knew my chances of winning were higher. But if most of their materials came from one company, I knew it would be a tougher fight.

When I sold instruments, I would assess the age of their existing equipment. If everything was less than five years old, that told me they liked to stay current and invest in new technology. But if their instruments looked outdated or were from companies that had gone out of business, I knew the road ahead would be steep.

Building relationships wasn't just about shaking hands and collecting business cards. It was about actually getting to know people. After meetings, I would follow up with emails or handwritten notes. Depending on who I was talking to, I would suggest grabbing coffee or lunch the next time I was in town. Those small touches made a big difference.

What you have just read is a masterclass in what I call becoming sticky. It is about focusing on the people, the products, and the processes inside your customer's organization. When you do that, you are better equipped to ask the right questions, stay curious, and step fully into their world.

And if you are reading this thinking, "I never leave my office to meet people," let me make it plain. You are a field or outside salesperson. That means it is time to get outside and go sell.

Pains Don't Sell, Problems Do

In sales, we always hear, "Find the pain points. Uncover the prospect's pain and solve it."

But here's the truth. Pains? They're annoying, but people don't fix annoying things unless they have to. We put a Band-Aid on it, deal with it, and move on. We don't jump to solve something unless it becomes a real problem.

Let me give you an example. As I'm writing this sentence, I've hit the 12,000-word mark on this book. That means I've typed 12,000 words in just a few days. Last night, I was deep in the zone typing away when my wrist started hurting. I ignored it for about 15 minutes, but it got worse. So, I shut my laptop and called it a day. This morning, my wrist feels better. Not perfect, but I'll take more breaks today to keep it from flaring up.

Now here's the thing: I don't have a hard deadline. I've set my own goal for when I want this rough draft done, but if it takes a few more days, it won't hurt me. That wrist pain? It was annoying, but not enough to force me into action beyond taking a break.

But let's flip the situation. Imagine I got a huge advance from a publisher, and I had to turn in 15,000 words by midnight. If I missed the deadline, they'd pull their money and support. Do you think I would've stopped 3,000 words short because of a sore wrist? Absolutely not. I'd have powered through the pain and kept typing.

Now, picture this. Right when my wrist starts acting up, a pain specialist knocks on my door. They're in the neighborhood, and of course, I'd chat with them because I love talking to salespeople. A few minutes into the conversation, they find out I'm writing a book and had to stop for the night because of my wrist. They offer me their magical, instant wrist pain relief for $10.

But at that moment, I'd probably say no. My wrist was annoying, but it wasn't bad enough to spend money on. I felt like I got enough done for the day, and I wasn't under pressure to keep going.

Now, let's say that same specialist showed up while I was racing to meet that deadline. Same wrist pain, same magical solution, but this time they're charging $100. Do you think I'd hesitate? Not for a second. I'd hand over the money without blinking. That wrist pain wasn't just annoying anymore—it was standing between me and losing thousands of dollars.

Here's the point. Pain is just annoying. Problems impact people, teams, and entire organizations. It's your job to dig past the annoyances and uncover the real problems. The ones that matter. The ones they have to fix.

The Hidden Problems Behind Every Pain

Problems aren't just pains—they're pains that have gotten deeper. They're the real issues your prospects are thinking about but not saying out loud.

As a salesperson, you're taught to find the pain and run with it because that's what your product fixes. We fix pains. Simple. But while you're busy focusing on that pain, your prospect is worrying about the problem. The bigger issues that hit the business and, more importantly, them personally.

Let's ditch the theory and get into some real examples:

- A company facing a 20 percent workforce cut if profits don't increase next quarter.
- A team struggling with high turnover that's wrecking productivity.
- A patent expiring in 12 months that's been responsible for 85 percent of revenue for nearly two decades.
- A manufacturing plant battling supply chain shortages that are driving up production costs.
- A professor up for tenure who hasn't hit the milestones needed to secure it.

Now, have you ever had a prospect lead with something like this? Probably not. But these are the things keeping them up at night. This is what they actually care about—not the product you're pitching.

In the last chapter, I had you identify your internal champion. Now it's time to figure out the specific problems they're dealing with. If you did that exercise right, you should be ready to call three of your internal champions and dig in. And no, don't call the same people you talked to before.

The insights you draw from these conversations are gold. You're stepping into the mind of the person you want to sell to, where you learn about their biggest frustrations, their challenges, and their goals. And from here on out, everything you do—your conversations, your emails, your content—should speak their language, not yours. Focus on what matters to them.

But here's the thing: identifying the problem isn't enough. To close the deal, you need to connect those problems to impacts. This is where everything comes together. It's not just about knowing what's wrong—you need to understand how it's affecting them, both at work and in their personal life.

Understanding Impacts: The Missing Link in Sales

Impacts are the real-world consequences of the pains and problems your prospects are dealing with. Pain is annoying. Problems mess with processes. But impacts? Impacts hit where it matters most—the bottom line and the personal stakes. They show how these issues affect the company's revenue, efficiency, and future, and how they impact the people involved—their stress, job security, and even their personal lives.

Understanding impacts changes the entire sales conversation. When you tie your solution directly to a business or personal consequence, you stop being just another salesperson. You become the person who can fix things. You're not pitching features and benefits—you're showing exactly how your solution changes their situation.

Let's say your product improves manufacturing efficiency. That's great, but it's just a feature until you connect it to the impact:

Business Impact: "Improving efficiency reduces downtime, saving your company $500,000 a year in lost production."

Personal Impact: "With fewer production issues, your team doesn't have to work overtime to meet deadlines, which means less stress and better work-life balance."

When you highlight both the business and personal impacts, your solution becomes impossible to ignore.

Examples of Business and Personal Impacts

Let's revisit the problems we covered earlier and break them down into impacts.

- Problem: A company will have to cut 20 percent of its workforce if profits don't increase next quarter.
- Business Impact: Lower productivity, damaged morale, and a hit to the company's reputation.
- Personal Impact: The manager in charge of cost-cutting is worried about losing their own job if they can't prevent layoffs.

- Problem: A team is dealing with high turnover.
- Business Impact: Increased hiring and training costs, lost knowledge, and project delays.
- Personal Impact: The team leader is overwhelmed, constantly onboarding new people, and struggling to hit targets.

- Problem: A patent that generates 85 percent of revenue is expiring in 12 months.
- Business Impact: Huge revenue loss, potential investor pullout, and a shrinking market share.
- Personal Impact: The exec team feels pressure from shareholders, and the R&D head is scrambling to develop a replacement.

- Problem: A manufacturing plant is facing supply chain shortages that are driving up costs.
- Business Impact: Reduced profit margins, missed deadlines, and strained supplier relationships.
- Personal Impact: The plant manager is stressed, juggling complaints from both execs and customers.

- Problem: A professor up for tenure hasn't hit the required milestones.
- Business Impact: The university risks losing a key faculty member, which can hurt student satisfaction and the program's reputation.
- Personal Impact: The professor feels anxious, with career growth and financial stability on the line.

Uncovering Problems and Impacts in Conversations

You've found the pains, but now it's time to dig deeper. To uncover the real issues, the problems and their impacts, you need to ask the right questions. Here's how you move from surface-level pains to meaningful conversations that lead to sales.

Problem-Focused Questions:

1. What are {company's} top business goals for the next 12 months?
2. What role do you play in helping {company} achieve those goals?
3. As a {title}, what are your main responsibilities?
4. Which of those responsibilities eats up most of your time, energy, and budget?
5. Over the past year, what have been your biggest challenges?
6. Which challenges did you solve, and how? What changed after solving them?
7. For the challenges you didn't solve, what's been the result?

Impact-Focused Questions:

1. How is this issue affecting your team's ability to hit its goals?
2. What's the financial cost if this problem drags on for another quarter?
3. How is this challenge hitting you personally? More stress? Longer hours?
4. If this doesn't get fixed, what's the risk to the company? What's the risk to you?
5. How would solving this problem change things for you and your team?
6. These questions help shift the conversation from surface-level issues to what really matters. They connect the dots between pain, problem, and impact—and that's where the urgency to buy comes from.

In your supplemental materials, you'll find a table outlining pains, problems, and impacts. This final column is where you capture how these issues affect your prospect both professionally and personally. Be specific. The more detailed you are, the easier it is to tailor your message and close the deal.

Remember, pains are just the start. Problems crank the pain up. But impacts? They're what make people act. When you tie your solution to a clear, undeniable impact, you're not just selling; you're solving something that matters.

Writing this book has been such a rewarding experience, and I feel like we're embarking on this journey of self-discovery together. As we lean into customer-centric, problem-focused selling, we've covered a lot of ground. My hope is that you're already putting these concepts into practice as we move forward.

Now, let's dive into prospecting. It's much more than just dialing for dollars or handing out brochures. To truly become a prospecting powerhouse, you need to tap into three key pillars: networking, education, and direct methods. These pillars are the foundation of a strategy that goes beyond the basics, helping you connect more effectively with the right prospects.

BELIEF Selling™ in Action: Shifting from Pain to Real-World Impact

In this chapter, we see the BELIEF framework come to life through the story of uncovering the real problem behind a prospect's pain. By understanding not only the pain but also the impact, you can solve issues that truly matter and move your sales process forward.

B | Break Barriers

- Dig past surface-level pain points and uncover the deeper, more impactful problems.
- Challenge your assumptions and look beyond quick fixes to understand the full scope of the issue.

E | Embrace Growth

- Be curious about the bigger problems your prospect is facing.
- Focus on solutions that address the root cause, not just the symptoms, for lasting impact.

L | Learn Skills

- Always seek to understand the evolving challenges your prospect faces to stay relevant.
- Use each conversation as an opportunity to learn more about their business and their pain points.

I | Implement Boldly

- Confidently present your solution, showing how it directly addresses both the problem and its impact.
- Take action quickly after identifying the solution, showing urgency and commitment to solving their issues.

E | Execute Consistently
- Regularly evaluate and refine your approach to ensure you're continuously uncovering real problems and impacts.
- Maintain steady, consistent communication with your prospects to build long-term trust.

F | Fuel Others
- Share your insights and solutions, empowering your prospects to take action on solving their own problems.
- Create a culture of collaboration by learning from others, both inside and outside of your sales team, to further refine your solutions.
- By implementing these principles, you'll create stronger relationships, identify the real problems, and deliver solutions that make a significant difference for your clients.

CHAPTER 8

Mastering Prospecting: Turning Effort Into Results

Just like many salespeople, I didn't have a marketing team backing me up. I was solely responsible for prospecting. I did the cold calling, attended events, and hunted for leads all on my own. That struggle taught me one thing: successful prospecting is about persistence and creativity, not waiting for others to fill the funnel.

Now, maybe your situation is different. Perhaps you have a top-tier marketing team and an inside sales group that floods your inbox with leads every day. Or maybe you're focused on a few key accounts and don't need to worry about prospecting at all.

Before you skip this chapter, let me ask you a couple of questions:

Are you truly satisfied with the quality of your inbound leads?

Do you get 100 percent of your product orders from your key accounts?

If you answered "no" to either of these, then you need to keep reading. In this chapter, we're going to dive into the three pillars of prospecting.

> *Reimagining prospecting means focusing on quality over quantity.*

But here's the thing: every prospecting effort must be focused on targeting our internal champions. Remember, everything we do is part of building a solid foundation. If you haven't yet pinpointed who your champion is and what problems they're facing, you're not quite ready to prospect effectively.

Reimagining Prospecting: Quality Over Quantity

In recent years, the term "prospecting" has become synonymous with cold calling, cold emailing, and spamming on social media. I call these the "spray and pray" methods. The focus here is on the quantity of interactions through a few channels, rather than the quality of those interactions through multiple methods.

From now on, we're ditching the spray and pray approach. Deal?

To prospect effectively, you need to focus on three key areas—networking, educating, and using direct methods. Within each of these areas, there are numerous strategies to target your internal champion. By the end of this chapter, you'll have at least 12 different ways to prospect effectively!

Strategic Networking: Where to Focus Your Efforts

Let's start by clearing up a common misconception: networking is not the same as network marketing. They are two completely different things. Networking is about showing up at events, locations, or activities where your internal champion is likely to be.

Attending large events where you're surrounded by dozens of competitors doesn't help you cut through the noise. At those events, you're just one of 20 vendors offering the same thing. While events like these can be useful for brand awareness and staying relevant, they shouldn't take up more than 20 percent of your event calendar each year.

Tradeshows are one of the most well-known networking opportunities, but your goal should be to seek out smaller, more regional shows where your internal champion is likely to be. Instead of going to the National Association of Mechanical Engineers Conference, for example, look for a local or regional version of that same show.

At smaller events, fewer people attend, but that gives you more chances to connect with everyone there and set up one-on-one meetings before, during, or after the show.

I used to dread tradeshows as a salesperson. Sitting behind a booth for three days, having small talk with random passersby—it felt like a huge waste of time. But I decided that if I had to spend a week in a random city, I was going to make it worth my while.

Instead of just showing up with a flashy banner and brochures, I became intentional. I started reaching out to my internal champions ahead of time, letting them know about the show and inviting them to meet. This gave me two major benefits: first, I was providing value by informing them about an event they might not have considered, and second, I knew I would be having meaningful conversations during the week.

I also started submitting abstracts to speak at shows. This wasn't just about getting in front of an audience. It was about positioning myself as an expert and building credibility with my internal champions. When you're the one leading a session, people listen differently. It helped me stand out and start meaningful conversations instead of waiting for someone to stumble by my booth.

I also made it a point to attend my competitors' sessions. This gave me insight into what they were offering, how they were positioning themselves, and what kind of value they were bringing to their audience. It wasn't just about spying; it was about learning how to differentiate myself and understand my competition better.

On top of that, I started organizing customer appreciation events during the show. These events weren't just for show; they were an opportunity to build stronger relationships with existing clients, gather feedback, and identify new needs that I could help solve. It was a way to deepen trust while also setting the stage for new opportunities.

Finally, I started doing live demos at my booth. Instead of just handing out brochures and hoping for the best, I engaged people directly, showing them how our product worked and how it could solve their specific problems. This helped me stand out from the crowd and create more targeted, valuable conversations.

By implementing all of these strategies, tradeshows went from a time-wasting obligation to one of my most valuable sources of leads. One good show would lead to 5-10 closed deals within 90 days. These tactics not only made the events more productive, but they also helped me build stronger relationships with internal champions and clients. This means that I saw a direct return on my time and effort. As a result, tradeshows went from being a total time-suck to one of my most reliable sources of leads. One solid show could lead to five to ten closed deals within 90 days.

Industry events are another great way to network. These are similar to tradeshows but are focused on specific industries. Instead of being surrounded by people with the same title as your internal champion, you'll find industry professionals who are connected to your top clients.

For instance, if you specialize in pharmaceutical manufacturing, particularly injectables, you might attend a niche event focusing on injectable pharmaceuticals for animals. Here, you'll find people who are deeply interested in the same areas of manufacturing, and you'll likely meet new internal champions or discover problems your champions are facing that you can solve.

Another great option is the local Chamber of Commerce. Chambers are private, nonprofit organizations focused on growing businesses in a specific city. They host events year-round that you can attend.

Now, before you roll your eyes and assume these events are just for insurance agents and financial advisors, let me share a story. A salesperson in New Mexico attended one of these Chamber events after a training I led. The topic was about new high-speed internet regulations in rural areas. This salesperson just happened to sell network cabling. After the talk, they stuck around and casually chatted with people about the new regulations and their impact on local businesses.

They ended up talking to a business owner who needed to upgrade all of their equipment to meet the new regulations. By the end of the week, the salesperson had a meeting scheduled. Within 30 days, they closed a deal to upgrade not just one building, but three.

The key here? The salesperson understood their internal champion's potential challenges, found the right event to attend, and simply started a conversation.

Finally, let's talk about networking groups. These fall into two categories: groups where your internal champions are and groups where your ideal referral partners show up.

Building a network of referral partners is critical. These are people who work with your internal champions, but in non-competing industries. For example, if you sell commercial cleaning services, companies that supply cleaning products or provide electrical maintenance are excellent referral partners.

Look for both in-person and virtual networking groups to join. But make sure you do your homework first. Some organizations put too much pressure on members to generate leads at every meeting, but a strong referral group is about giving and receiving value. Think of opportunities like sharing a trade show booth with a partner.

If you can't find the right group in your area, start your own.

For the networking pillar, if you're a full-time salesperson, aim to attend at least one event per month. If you have other responsibilities outside of sales, aim for six events each year.

> **A strong referral group is about giving and receiving value.**

Teaching to Win: The Art of Educating Your Prospects

Simply put, educate them, and they will come. The more you teach your prospects, the more they'll look to you as a trusted advisor.

But let's be clear: education is not about dumping your entire product knowledge onto their heads. It's not about showing up, talking about your company, and listing all the reasons why you're great. Education is about focusing on your prospect's problems and providing them with resources to solve them.

Customer-centric, problem-oriented education is the goal of everything you create in this pillar. Before we dive into the types of educational content or events to create, let's talk about how to come up with the right topics.

Start by referring back to the table you created with your internal champions' pains, problems, and impacts. If you haven't done that exercise yet, make sure you complete at least three interviews before moving forward with this pillar of prospecting.

The problems and pains your clients share with you should be the foundation of your educational prospecting plan. Each problem represents something they need help solving or a challenge they want to brainstorm solutions for. So, let's give them an outlet for that.

In my first sales job, I was responsible for a massive territory called 'Intermountain.' It spanned from Texas up to the Dakotas, over to Montana, and down to New Mexico. I had no point of reference at the time, so I thought all salespeople had such large territories.

It became clear pretty quickly that if I didn't want to spend 300 days a year in a hotel, I needed to find a way to reach the remote areas of my territory more effectively. That's when I decided to do at least one Lunch and Learn in each state every month.

This approach became a strategy I still teach sales reps today because it works so well—and they don't need much support from their company to execute it.

You can hold company-specific Lunch and Learns or open events for the public. For a company-specific one, simply call up your internal champion, let them know you'll be in town, and ask if they think it would be helpful to gather a few colleagues to discuss one of the problems you know is on their company's mind.

All they need to do is reserve a room and invite anyone who might be interested, or even just want a free lunch. A few days before the event, confirm the headcount and order box lunches. Box lunches are quick and easy, allowing you to dive straight into the content.

For a public event, make sure the location is neutral. Depending on your budget, you could host it at a public library or university for free or at a low cost. If you're at a university, you'll need an internal champion to help book the room for you. If you have the budget, renting a conference room for a few hours is also a solid option.

Your Lunch and Learn should last no longer than 90 minutes. Be sure to allow time for questions and discussion. The key to a successful event is going deep on one topic. For example, if your company helps find tax credits for organizations, don't overwhelm them with information on the 50 credits they could be eligible for. Focus on one or two that will truly grab their attention.

At the end of the session, you can drop in a very soft pitch for your company. And I emphasize at the end—don't start with a 10-minute sales pitch. You'll lose the audience right away.

The same principle applies to half-day or full-day seminars. Just be sure you're going deep on a subject instead of trying to cover everything under the sun. You don't have to be the subject matter expert when presenting educational content. Your role as the salesperson is to plan the event. You can get someone from your technical support, engineering, or operations teams to deliver the presentation.

If planning in-person events feels like too much or is outside your budget, consider webinars. You can apply the same principles, but limit webinars to 60 minutes per session. It's better to have a series of three 60-minute webinars over a few weeks than one three-hour session—people's attention will wander, and you'll lose them.

Written forms of educational content, like e-books, blogs, or white papers, are also effective. The goal is the same as with spoken content—offering subject matter expertise on your prospects' problems in a format they can refer back to and use as a short guide.

For instance, creating an eBook titled "The Top Ten Pitfalls to Avoid When Preparing for a Scheduled Plant Shutdown" will attract attention from a VP of Operations. If you're targeting academic institutions, a white paper will resonate with them because they're constantly reading and writing for academic journals.

Another great strategy is interviews, both interviews where you're being interviewed and interviews with your happy customers. Podcasts and YouTube videos are popular ways for people to stay updated in their fields, and content creators are always looking for interesting people to interview. You are that interesting person. Do a quick Google search for 'podcasts your internal champion listens to' and reach out to the hosts to ask if you can be a guest. Once the episode is live, you can use it in your sales process.

Finally, interview your current clients. These testimonial interviews are valuable because they walk you through their pains, problems, impacts, and the solution you helped them achieve. Always do these interviews via video; this way, you can use the full video, cut it into pieces, and even turn the transcript into a written case study.

As a full-time salesperson, your goal is to have at least six educational events in your territory each year. If you have other responsibilities outside of sales, aim for four.

The Power of Direct Prospecting: Moving Beyond Cold Calls

This is the pillar where most salespeople spend the majority of their time. Traditionally, we've been taught to cold call and cold email to fill the top of our funnel. A cold call means we know nothing about the person we're calling. We simply pick up our virtual phone book, type in "design engineers in Chicago," and start calling and emailing.

That ends now. Deal?

We're transitioning from cold calling and emailing to warm calling and emailing. The difference? We've profiled our ideal internal champion, and we know exactly who to target. Instead of calling all design engineers, we'll focus on those who've been in their positions for less than three years because that's where our top customers fit.

No more sending generic emails about how great our company is, loaded with brochures and asking for a time to meet. Instead, we'll focus on the pains and problems our internal champions are facing and offer one solution that helps them solve those challenges.

We won't send long, text-heavy emails that no one will read. Every email will be concise, with plenty of white space to make it easy for the reader.

When we email prospects, our focus will remain customer-centric and problem-focused. In your sales reset guide, you'll find a step-by-step guide on how to write warm emails. I used this exact formula to close a six-figure deal as a sales trainer. After just two warm emails, a discovery call, and a proposal meeting, the deal was closed. The person I met gushed, "I want all my salespeople to send emails like you." So, when you're ready, flip to the back and try your hand at writing some rock-solid emails.

Each week, you should set a goal for how many emails and calls you'll make to brand new prospects. Every sales situation is different, and I don't want to put you in a box. But generally, somewhere between five and 20 is where you should fall. Five is ideal for those with an established book of business, and 20 is a good goal for someone new to sales.

Yes, you'll send more than five emails a week, but that number represents emails specifically targeting new prospects or people you want to extract more business from.

Social media prospecting is a method that could fill an entire book on its own. If you've made it this far, you may spend most of your time in the field with clients and think social media won't help you close deals.

But here is the key. Social media prospecting is all about supporting your prospects' individual posts or company updates. A simple like and a thoughtful comment shows up in their notifications, so when your email lands in their inbox, there is already a spark of recognition.

You do not need to post every day. Once or twice a month is enough to stay visible. But do make it a habit to spend at least 30 minutes a week engaging with your prospects' content. That could be liking their posts, commenting with a perspective, or sharing something relevant to their role or industry.

Most people get a few likes and zero comments on their posts. By being the first to comment, you're stepping into their world and showing support for whatever they're talking about. It costs you nothing, but it creates a moment of connection they remember.

Why does this work? Because my top clients never comment or like any of my posts. Not once. But when we talk, they reference something I said in a post from weeks ago. That tells me, and it should tell you, that they are watching. They are reading. Even when they are silent, they are listening.

And this is where personal branding becomes more than a buzzword.

Your personal brand on LinkedIn is your digital handshake. It is often the first impression a prospect has of you. Before they respond to your message, they are checking your profile. They are reading your posts. They are deciding if you sound like someone who understands their world or someone who is just trying to sell.

When you share content that reflects your values, your expertise, and your perspective on the industry, you become more than just a rep. You become a trusted voice. Your profile should not just say what you sell. It should show who you are, who you help, and what you believe.

Sales is personal. Therefore, your presence online should match the professionalism and passion you bring in person.

So if you have been lurking, it is time to start leading. Your prospects are already on LinkedIn. The question is, are you showing up in a way that makes them want to learn more?

The final part of directed prospecting involves offline methods—showing up unannounced and sending mailers.

When you plan a visit to an area, look up other potential targets in the area. Do your research before you go. When you show up, it shouldn't be the first time the person has heard your name. This should be someone you've met at an event, sent a few emails to, or interacted with on LinkedIn.

When you arrive, walk up to the reception desk and ask for the person by name. Of course, they're not expecting you, but there's a 50 percent chance they'll come to the lobby and chat with you. Sometimes, they might think they've forgotten about a meeting. You've got to be bold, but this method can work if you're willing to try it.

And if you bring food or some kind of treats, the chance of them coming down increases from 50 percent to 75 percent.

We get so much junk mail these days. When was the last time you received a handwritten note or a book from a vendor with notes on their favorite chapters attached? Trust me, your internal champions aren't getting anything of real value in the mail.

To cut through the noise, send something thoughtful that they'll actually value. Maybe you saw them in a picture on the golf course online—send them a few golf balls. Or maybe, during your initial conversation, they mentioned updating their CRM. If you've just read a great book on increasing CRM usage, send it to them.

These direct methods are much more intentional and should be part of your prospecting process. Each week, make sure you're involved in at least one of these activities.

The ultimate goal of prospecting is simple: getting that first meeting. You'll know your prospecting efforts are working when your calendar starts filling up with meetings, both with brand new clients and with existing clients who are eager to do business with you again.

When I became intentional about following my prospecting plan, I'd often find my calendar booked out for six weeks at a time.

Now that the top of your funnel is full, it's time to step into the next phase: the meetings. But what do you say in these meetings? And how can you determine if the person you're talking to is actually qualified to buy?

In the next chapter, we'll dive into discovery meetings and qualification, two crucial steps that will help you identify which prospects are worth your time and energy.

BELIEF Selling™ in Action: Driving Consistent Results Through Prospecting

As you move forward with the strategies from this chapter, it's time to put them into action. These takeaways will help you break barriers, stay focused, and execute your prospecting efforts with purpose. By embracing each step, you'll consistently build stronger connections and fill your pipeline with quality opportunities. Let's put these insights into motion and make your prospecting efforts work for you.

B | Break Barriers

- Shift from traditional cold calling and cold emailing to intentional, quality interactions.
- Let go of the "spray and pray" approach and focus on solving your prospects' problems.
- Embrace strategically targeted prospecting and break free from old habits.

E | Embrace Growth

- Take control of your sales funnel by focusing on warm, relationship-driven prospecting.
- Recognize your internal champions as the key to opportunities and prioritize the right people.
- Understand that prospecting is about building relationships and addressing customer needs, which will help guide each interaction with confidence.

L | Learn Skills

- Master the pillars of networking, educating, and direct prospecting by continuously learning.
- Refine your email strategies, attend targeted events, and engage on social media to keep evolving your approach.

- Adapt to the ever-changing world of prospecting by constantly adjusting and improving your methods.

I | Implement Boldly

- Take proactive action—don't wait for inbound leads.
- Reach out, attend events, set up meetings, and engage with prospects confidently.
- Boldly implement strategies that align with your champion-focused approach and make intentional connections.

E | Execute Consistently

- Stay consistent in executing your prospecting plan, whether it's sending emails, attending events, or engaging on social media.
- Set daily, weekly, and monthly goals to keep your pipeline full and your sales efforts on track.
- Consistency is the key to building sustained results.

F | Fuel Others

- Share the knowledge and strategies you've learned to elevate the success of those around you.
- Teach your team the power of intentional prospecting through mentoring, hosting Lunch and Learns, and leading by example.
- Inspire and empower others to adopt effective prospecting practices, fueling growth within your team.

CHAPTER 9

Diagnose Before You Prescribe: The Power of Discovery

My biggest pet peeve? Sitting on the other side of the sales table while someone pitches at me nonstop without asking a single meaningful question.

Even worse? Walking into a meeting where I've been misled from the very start.

Let me tell you about a time that still makes my blood boil.

A company reached out saying a major media outlet was looking for voices like mine to contribute to a national article. I was intrigued. Writing is one of my passions. Sharing expertise is what I do. I was excited and honored to be considered.

But that excitement didn't last.

Before the meeting, I got six reminder emails. Not confirmations. Reminders. That was the first red flag. I already felt like an item on a checklist, not a person being invited into something valuable.

> *Sales malpractice happens when you prescribe before you diagnose.*

Then I joined the call, and everything unraveled.

The person I scheduled with wasn't there. Someone else showed up. And that person wasn't even listed on the invite. No explanation. No context. Just, "Hi, I'm here to talk with you today."

After a few minutes of surface-level small talk, they asked, "So what are your public relations goals?"

That's when I knew. This wasn't what they promised. There was no article. No editorial opportunity. Just a cold pitch disguised as something it wasn't.

I said, "I don't have PR goals. You told me this was about contributing to a story."

Then came the truth. "We get hundreds of media inquiries a day. We help clients gain visibility through strategic partnerships."

That was it. The mask came off. I had been baited.

They lied to get me in the room.

Let me be clear. This wasn't just a bad experience. It was a betrayal. And it is one of the most toxic habits in sales today—getting someone on a call under false pretenses and calling it a strategy.

Here's what they missed: Discovery is the most sacred part of the sales process. That is where you learn who this person is, what they need, and if you can actually help.

But they never earned the right to ask me anything. They skipped the most important step—earning trust.

If they had been honest from the start, maybe I would have listened. Maybe we could have had a real conversation about visibility or media strategy. But they never gave me the chance.

That's what happens when you lie to get the meeting. You show up to sell, but the buyer shows up guarded. The wall is already up. The opportunity is already gone.

Your sale begins and ends in discovery. And if your prospect feels deceived before you even ask the first question, nothing else you say will matter.

You only get one chance to make someone feel safe enough to tell you the truth. If you blow that, the deal is already dead.

Sales Malpractice: Diagnose Before You Prescribe

Before we dive into what you should say or the information you need to gather in a meeting, let's address the foundational truths that apply to every single discovery meeting. But first, what exactly is a discovery meeting?

A discovery meeting is exactly what it sounds like. It is a meeting to discover more about your prospects. More specifically, it's about uncovering the pains, problems, and impacts your prospect is facing.

Think about this for a moment. If you show up with a stack of cookie-cutter slides, how will you ever assess the unique challenges your prospects are dealing with?

Let me paint a picture for you. You've been battling an annoying cough for weeks, staying up late consulting "Dr. Google," convincing yourself it's something serious. Finally, you decide to see a real doctor. When scheduling the appointment, you tell the receptionist about your persistent cough.

The next day, you walk into the doctor's office, expecting answers. Instead, the doctor has a generic image of lungs on the screen. Without listening to your lungs or even examining you, he launches into a speech about being a five-time award-winning pulmonary specialist. He name-drops his high-profile patients and lists all the advanced techniques he's mastered.

After 20 minutes of rambling, he finally looks at you and says, "Based on my experience, you have a small mass growing in your lungs. It's not life-threatening, but I've already written prescriptions and scheduled surgery for tomorrow at eight a.m."

When he's done, he asks if you have any questions. But after that overwhelming display of ego, you feel too intimidated to challenge him. So, you nod quietly, pretending to agree.

Later that afternoon, you call the office to cancel the surgery and toss the prescriptions in the trash.

For the next three weeks, the doctor bombards you with calls, emails, and texts. You ignore every single one. You never see that doctor again, and when anyone asks, you tell them to find someone else.

Sounds outrageous, right? That scenario would never happen in real life. It's medical malpractice to prescribe treatment without a proper diagnosis, and sharing other patients' records is a serious violation.

But here's the thing. When you show up to a discovery meeting and start pitching before understanding your prospect's underlying problems, you're committing sales malpractice.

Let's make a pact right now: "From this day forward, I will no longer make discovery meetings about me and my company. I will focus on a full diagnosis before recommending any solutions."

A strong discovery meeting isn't about how much you talk. It's about how much they talk. Aim to speak for 25 percent of the time or less. In a 30-minute meeting, that means you're talking for eight minutes or less. The more your prospect talks, the more successful your meeting will be.

Your job is simple. Have one powerful question ready to open the conversation, then follow your prospect's lead. Yes, you'll ask other questions, but each one should be based on what the prospect just told you. When you do speak, reflect back what you've heard. Show them you're listening, not just waiting for your turn to talk.

We begin our discovery meetings with broad, open-ended questions because our goal is to step into their world.

To truly understand the problems they're experiencing, we must first listen deeply, diagnose accurately, and only then offer solutions that actually matter.

During a discovery meeting, your primary aim should be to understand their pains and problems before jumping into solutions. This is why we use a framework called DIVE DEEP Discovery™ to guide our conversations.

DIVE DEEP Discovery™: The Cure for Sales Malpractice

DIVE is an acronym we will use to categorize the types of questions you should ask in discovery meetings. For our purposes, DIVE stands for Dig, Investigate, Validate, Echo.

Let's break them down one at a time.

Dig means exactly what it sounds like—to go deeper. Move below the surface level of what your prospect offers you. A strong dig question makes your prospect pause and think. When they say, "That's a good question, no one has ever asked me that before," you know you've struck gold.

DIVE DEEP questions are designed to uncover problems. These are the challenges your prospect faces that may not be immediately obvious. By digging deeper, you bring these hidden issues to the surface.

Here's how you set up a good dig question. This requires doing a bit of research and knowing your prospect's current situation.

> *Discovery should create clarity, not pressure.*

Examples:

"I noticed your company recently acquired a smaller competitor. How has this shift impacted the day-to-day responsibilities or morale of your team?"

"As we walked through the plant, I noticed a few pieces of equipment were not being used. Can you share with me why, and how that affects your operations?"

Start with knowledge you've gained from research or observation, then dig into the reasons why. Dig questions should always be open-ended. If you can answer the question with one word, it's closed-ended and not serving the purpose.

Investigate questions are open-ended, process-oriented questions. They help you understand the "how." When you ask investigate questions, you're looking for a step-by-step walk-through of something. You might ask these to find gaps in how they produce a product or to understand the process for becoming a new vendor.

These questions are crucial because they let you step fully into the prospect's world and understand how they operate.

Investigate questions help uncover pain points. These are the frustrations and inefficiencies in their processes that cause daily headaches. It's your job to identify these pain points and understand their root causes.

Examples:

"Can you walk me through the process you use to onboard new clients? Where do you find the process tends to slow down or become more complicated?"

"Can you share the steps an engineer follows to create a new design? Are there any steps that seem to cause delays or frustrations?"

Pay close attention to what they say—and what they don't say. You can glean valuable information from what they emphasize or gloss over and from any frustration they express about difficult processes.

Validate questions drill down into the precise information you need to craft the right solution for your clients. Most of the time, prospects won't offer this up on their own. These are great follow-ups to dig or investigate questions. When you notice something they're passionate or frustrated about, you need to get specific.

These questions are critical for identifying the impact of the problems and pain points. By understanding the tangible effects—whether financial, operational, or emotional—you can better tailor your solution to meet their needs.

Examples:

"When you shared the steps engineers use to create a new design, I noticed you mentioned Bob and Ryan use different processes. Can you share the difference in their final products and how that impacts your overall workflow or quality?"

"You mentioned three pieces of equipment that have been out of service for six months. How has this downtime affected your production targets or revenue goals?"

Here, you're looking for facts, figures, and numbers—the details that will help you build a tailored solution.

Echo questions are the only closed-ended questions you should use in a discovery meeting. Prospects want to know you're listening, and when you repeat back what they've shared, it encourages them to open up even more.

To use an echo question, summarize what you've heard and ask them to validate it.

Examples:

"I want to make sure I'm capturing everything you shared. {{Summarize what you heard}}. Am I on the right track?"

"You mentioned these are the steps you've taken to resolve the problem. {{Summarize what they shared}}. Did I miss anything?"

By using the DIVE Deep Discovery™ framework, you're ensuring that your discovery meetings are focused on understanding your prospect's true needs before offering any solutions. This approach ties directly back to avoiding sales malpractice. Just like a doctor would never prescribe treatment without a proper diagnosis, you should never pitch a solution without fully understanding the prospect's challenges, processes, and specific needs. Following DIVE keeps you in the diagnostic mindset, ensuring you provide value and build trust rather than rushing into a pitch that misses the mark.

How to Lose a Prospect with One Question

We've already talked about the right questions to ask during discovery. But just as important are the questions you should never ask. Yes, there is such a thing as a bad question. And asking the wrong one can derail your entire sales process, shut your prospect down, and cost you the deal before you even realize it.

Let's break down three types of bad questions—and what to ask instead.

1. Complex Questions: Too Much, Too Fast

Asking two or more questions at once overwhelms your prospect. They will only answer the one that feels safest, which means you miss out on what really matters.

Avoid this:

"How does this process impact your timeline and budget?"

It's confusing and gets a surface-level answer.

Ask this instead:

"How does this process impact your timeline?"

Then ask, "And what effect has it had on your budget?"

One question at a time. Clear. Focused. Effective.

2. Leading Questions: Telling Instead of Learning

Leading questions show up when you assume you know the answer. You might be trying to sound informed, but instead, you come off as pushy or judgmental.

Avoid this:

"What do you think is the reason your parts are coming out bad?"

You just assumed the outcome is bad before they've even explained the process.

Ask this instead:

"I noticed some parts set aside in quality control. Can you walk me through what you're seeing there?"

Stay curious. Let them define the problem in their own words.

3. Pushy Questions: The Fast Track to Getting Ghosted

These questions focus more on your quota than their needs.

Avoid these:

"What keeps you up at night?"

"What's your budget?"

"Are you the decision maker?"

"When do you plan to place the order?"

These make your prospect feel like a transaction, not a person.

The things that keep someone up at night? None of your business.

Budget? They don't trust you enough to share that yet and asking too soon makes you look desperate.

Questioning their authority? You just slapped them in the face.

Asking when they'll place an order? Congratulations, you've officially become a quota-chaser.

These questions scream I only care about closing the deal and make your prospect feel like just another number. Nobody wants to feel like a transaction. The "used car salesperson" stereotype exists because of this high-pressure nonsense.

Ask this instead:

"What's most important to you when evaluating a solution like this?"

That question shows respect, gets to the heart of the decision, and keeps the door open for deeper conversation.

If you want your prospect to open up, you have to create a space where they feel heard, not hunted. Bad questions shut people down. Great ones open the door to trust.

Bad questions are all about you and what you need to make a sale. Good questions are about stepping into their world, understanding their challenges, and building trust.

Before you ask a question, pause and ask yourself:

Does this help me understand their world better? Or is this just about getting the info I need to build a quote?

The right questions open doors. The wrong ones? They'll have your prospect hitting "decline" the next time you call. Choose wisely.

You've got discovery down. Don't forget, every time a new stakeholder shows up, you redo discovery. No shortcuts. You need to understand their pains and problems, not just rely on what you already know. Keep those DIVE Deep Discovery™ questions focused on stepping into their world, not just collecting info to slap together a quote.

With discovery mastered, it's time to move the deal forward. In the next chapter, we'll dive into delivering demos and proposals that actually convert. And let me be clear: never combine your discovery meeting with a proposal or demo. Discovery is for gathering insights. Proposals and demos? That's where you prove you were paying attention. Let's go.

BELIEF Selling™ in Action: Mastering the Art of Discovery

Now that you understand the importance of discovery meetings and how to avoid common pitfalls, it's time to put the BELIEF framework into action. This isn't just about knowing what to do; it's about consistently applying these principles in every single interaction.

B | Break Barriers

- Let go of the belief that your value comes from how much you talk.
- Recognize that listening is your strongest tool.
- Challenge the idea that you need to "sell" during discovery. Focus on uncovering.

E | Empower Mindset

- Shift from "closing the deal" to "building trust."
- Understand that the best salespeople are the best listeners.
- Prioritize understanding over pitching to position yourself as a trusted advisor.

L | Learn Continuously

- Treat every discovery meeting as an opportunity to improve.
- Reflect after each meeting: Did I talk too much? Did I dig deep enough?
- Recognize that thinking you've got it all figured out is a growth killer.

I | Implement Boldly

- Don't just read about DIVE DEEP Discovery™ questions. Use them.
- Be ready to dig deeper, gain insight, get specific, and confirm in every meeting.

- Push through discomfort. Growth happens outside your comfort zone.

E | Execute Consistently

- Mastery comes from doing it right every single time, not just once.
- Prepare your questions before each meeting and review afterward.
- Make consistent execution an essential part of your process.

F | Fuel Others

- Sales isn't a solo game. Share what you've learned with your team.
- Partner with colleagues to compare notes and improve together.
- The more you help others grow, the stronger your sales culture becomes.

CHAPTER 10

Stop Selling on Price, Start Selling on Value

Never once in my sales career did I sell the cheapest product.

My first sales job was with a German company. One of the big selling points they drilled into me was "superior German engineering." But that didn't mean a thing to my prospects until they saw we were 30 percent more expensive than the competition.

I would send over a quote, and they would go line by line, picking it apart. They would ask why they needed certain features and why our price was so much higher than everyone else's.

Trying to close some business, I would go to my manager and ask for a discount. Most of the time, I would get ten to twenty percent approved, and the prospect would be satisfied. I would feel relieved and excited because I closed the deal.

Then the pattern started. When those same customers came back for spare parts or a service contract, they expected the same discount. I had set a precedent in their minds that they would never pay full price.

And because I was taught that the customer is always right, I kept discounting.

Then came the moment everything changed.

I had been working with a client for months. They bought an entry-level instrument from me, plus some accessories, all heavily discounted. As their business grew, so did their need for more equipment. I got their RFP and sent over a quote with their usual discount, assuming it was an easy win.

A few days went by. Nothing.

I called to follow up, expecting a purchase order. Instead, they told me they had placed the order with my competitor.

I was in shock. I had fought for them internally, pulled strings to get them better pricing, and made sure they had everything they needed.

When I asked why, the answer hit me like a gut punch. They went with them because they were two thousand dollars cheaper.

I was speechless. I had spent months building a relationship and bending over backward to accommodate them, and they chose to save two thousand dollars.

That was the moment it all clicked. This is what happens when you play the price game. When you win on price, you lose on price because you have not built value.

That was the day I vowed never to win on price again.

And once I made that shift, everything changed. I stopped chasing discounts and started selling real value. I went from being a transactional rep to a trusted advisor. And the best part? I started hitting my quota faster than ever because my focus was in the right place.

> *When you win on price, you lose on price.*

Mastering the Demo: Turning Features Into Value

When a prospect tells you they didn't move forward because your price was too high, eighty percent of the time that is not the real issue. It is not about the number on the quote. It is about the value you provided for that number. What they are really saying is that what you showed them was not worth what you are asking them to pay.

So how do you fix that?

The first step in building value is stepping into their world. You have to pull out their pains, their problems, and the impact those issues are having on their business. Then you have to connect their challenges directly to your solution.

Your job is to bridge the gap between where they are right now—the frustrations, the inefficiencies, the things they have just accepted as part of the job—versus where they could be with your solution. Most prospects do not even realize things can be better until you show them.

That is where the "show me" stage comes in. And no, this does not mean a feature dump. It means demonstrating exactly how your solution solves their specific problem.

The key to a good demo is focus. One problem, one solution. Do not overwhelm your prospect. You get five features or benefits. That is it.

Before you push back on that, let me show you what I mean.

Let's say during discovery you uncover that every shift change costs your prospect fifteen minutes of downtime. Three shifts a day means forty-five minutes lost daily. Over a month, that is one thousand three hundred fifty minutes, which adds up to twenty-seven hours of lost production. They are losing an entire workday every single month, and it is just happening because they do not know another way.

Your solution is a cloud-based software that lets employees sign in and out remotely, eliminating that lost time completely.

Now here is where most salespeople mess up.

They start showing everything. How to add employees. The setup process. All the extra bells and whistles. But the prospect does not care about any of that.

All they need to see is this: John logs off, Jane logs in, and the transition is seamless. That is it. That is the moment when they realize they do not have to lose twenty-seven hours a month anymore.

And when you present it, you do not just describe the feature. You tie it back to the pain you uncovered.

Do not say, "This feature lets employees log in and out easily."

Say this:

"One of the concerns you mentioned was losing fifteen minutes per shift during operator changes. That adds up to twenty-seven hours of lost production every month. This feature eliminates that completely. One person logs in while the other wraps up, keeping everything running. Before I move on, does this solve your biggest concern?"

That is how you take discovery insights and turn them into undeniable value.

Does it really matter how the system works behind the scenes? No. Does it matter what the company has to enter to make it work? No.

The only thing that matters is the output. The result.

When you present value this way, price stops being the problem.

Do not assume every sales conversation needs a demo. A bad demo can completely tank a deal. You can go from a solid opportunity to falling flat on your face.

So, when should you do a demo?

Here is when it makes sense:

- The customer asks to see the product.
- They use a competitor's product and have concerns about specific features.
- You are selling something new or breaking into a market where buyers are unfamiliar with what you offer.

Sometimes, live demos are not possible. Maybe you cover a huge territory, and travel is not realistic. That is not an excuse. Get creative. Do virtual demos from your home office. Have pre-recorded videos ready to go that highlight the features your prospects actually care about.

If you are a distributor, you might be thinking, "I can't do a demo." There are 50 line items from ten different vendors on this quote. No one is asking you to demo everything. That would be ridiculous.

But there is always one product or one vendor solving your prospect's biggest headache. That is what you focus on. Show them the part of your solution that actually matters to them. Nothing more. Nothing less.

Proposal Reviews Are Non-Negotiable

Demonstrations are optional. Proposal review meetings are not.

From this day forward, you will never email a quote or proposal to a new prospect again. You will always walk them through it in person or virtually. Always.

The whole premise of this book is stepping into your prospect's world. Sending a proposal without reviewing it forces them into your world. It is lazy selling. You are basically saying, "Here, figure out my random part numbers, internal jargon, and fine print on your own."

Proposal reviews are non-negotiable.

And guess what most prospects do? The same thing you and I do when we get a quote. Scroll straight to the bottom and look at the price. If the number seems fine, they might skim the rest. If it doesn't, they move on.

Sending a proposal without a review guarantees they focus only on the price. If they do not understand the reason behind what they are getting, they will never see the real value. And if they don't see the value, you are stuck in a transactional sale.

At the end of your discovery meeting or demo, schedule your proposal review. Do not let the conversation end without locking in the next step. Ask, "When works best for you to go through the proposal together?" If you leave it open-ended, you will be chasing them down later.

Many times, your prospect will ask for the pricing if you have done a good job getting them interested. When they do, your response is simple:

"Let's set up a quick meeting to make sure the solution I'm recommending meets your needs. That way, I can walk you through the details and answer any questions upfront. What day and time next week works best for you?"

If they push back, say:

"I want to make sure you are getting exactly what you need. A quick review helps avoid misunderstandings and ensures this is the right fit for your business."

But what if they insist that you email the proposal?

You do not need to push. You just need to guide the conversation.

Try this:

"I am happy to send it over. I just know from experience that without context, proposals often create more questions than answers. I would rather walk you through it live so we can ensure it speaks to what matters most to you."

If they still prefer the email, respect that while keeping the door open.

"Absolutely. I will send it over. If anything feels unclear or needs adjusting, I am here to walk through it together."

You are not chasing. You are leading. When you stay calm, clear, and helpful, you leave the door open for a real conversation. One that builds trust and keeps the deal moving.

Your Proposal Is a Conversation, Not a Monologue

This is not a one-sided presentation. It is a conversation. Keep it interactive. Pause and ask, "Does this align with what you need?" Stop and answer questions before moving on. Keep the focus on them.

When presenting a proposal, keep it simple. You do not need ten slides about why your company is great. No one cares. Stick to customer-centric, problem-focused selling.

Your proposal deck should start with a recap of the problems they shared with you, paired with the solutions you recommended. After each problem and solution, get agreement to ensure you are aligned.

Then, include two or three slides on why your company is the best partner for them. Not a list of awards. Not a history lesson. A strong, clear value proposition that ties back to what they need.

Finally, show their investment. If you can add a calculation for their return on investment, even better. And notice I said investment, not price. You are asking them to invest in change, not just buy a product.

After you walk through the proposal, ask for the sale.

Let me be clear about what that means.

Asking for the sale means inviting your prospect to take the next step with clarity and confidence. You are not begging. You are not pushing. You are simply guiding them toward a decision that you both know is aligned with their needs.

It sounds like:

"Based on everything we have discussed, I believe this solution is the right fit. Are you ready to move forward?"

Or

"Is there anything else you need to feel confident saying yes today?"

Asking for the sale is not about pressure. It is about partnership. It is the natural outcome of a process where you have built trust, uncovered real problems, and shown how your solution makes things better.

By this point, you should be talking to your internal champion and the rest of the decision committee. You should have already addressed objections and confirmed buy-in.

If you have done this right, there should be no price war. The value is clear. The relationship is strong. And the close becomes a conversation, not a battle.

You should get an easy yes.

If they hesitate, do not leave it hanging. Ask:

"I understand. Just so I can help you move this forward, what concerns do you still need to address?"

If they need to check with someone else, say:

"Great. When would be a good time for all of us to discuss it together? Let's set something up so I can answer any questions they might have."

This keeps the conversation moving instead of leaving you waiting for them to "get back to you."

When they say, "Everything looks great. What's the next step?" you tell them they will receive the official quote in their email within ten minutes and ask when you can expect a purchase order.

Just like that. Be bold. Ask for the order and get a commitment.

Does it sound too good to be true? It's not. You have put in the work. Every step of the process has filtered out unqualified prospects. By the time you reach this stage, your opportunity should be closable within 30 days.

And if it is not? Then you have more work to do earlier in the process.

The key shift in this process is to stop being transactional and step into the role of a trusted advisor. Because if you want to close more deals, you cannot just email a quote and hope they get it. You have to show them why it matters.

But to get here, we had to do the work. We had to make sure we were talking to the right person and asking the right questions. We had to fully step into the customer's world, pulling out their pains, problems, and the impact those issues were having. We had to run a demo that actually solved their problems instead of overwhelming them. And finally, we presented the proposal and got a verbal commitment.

> **The key shift in this process is to stop being transactional and step into the role of a trusted advisor.**

Y'all, we did it.

But maybe you are losing more than you are winning. Or maybe you are like I was at the beginning of this chapter—taking existing clients for granted and losing on price.

That story I shared? I lost a $75,000 deal over $2,000. And here is the kicker. The customer had only ever spent $30,000 with us over multiple months. I assumed they were loyal. I skipped discovery. I did not do a demo. I thought my past effort was enough.

It wasn't.

Sloppy, lazy selling got me sloppy, lazy results.

I am not going to call you sloppy or lazy, but I will tell you this. Be intentional. Every step of your sales process matters. If you do not take it seriously, your prospect won't either.

Your action steps for this chapter are to do effective demos and to build out your proposal deck. Because I am so gracious, and I want you to win more business quicker, I have included a template for you in the supplemental materials.

But what happens when things do not go as planned?

You ask the right questions. You run a solid demo. You walk them through the proposal. Then bam. Objections.

Price. Timing. Competitors. Internal red tape.

At every step, something is blocking the deal.

The good news is objections are not dealbreakers. They are just problems that need solving.

Next up, we are tackling the most common sales objections and how to handle them so you stay in control and keep the deal moving forward.

BELIEF Selling™ in Action: From Transactional to Trusted Advisor

B | Break Barriers

- Losing deals on price? It is not the number on the quote. It is how you positioned the value.
- If they do not see the value, that is on you.
- Stop assuming interest means they understand why your solution is worth the investment.

E | Embrace Growth

- The shift from transactional rep to trusted advisor changes everything.
- Your job is not to sell a product. Your job is to show them how their world gets better with your solution.
- You control that process. Do not leave it up to chance.

L | Learn Skills

- After every sales conversation, ask yourself:
- Did I dig deep enough in discovery, or did I just accept their first answer?
- Did I tailor my demo to their pain points, or did I do a generic feature dump?
- Did I walk them through the proposal and reinforce value, or did I let them skim straight to the price?
- The best salespeople never stop refining their approach.

I | Implement Boldly

- From now on, you will never send a proposal or quote without reviewing it. Ever.
- When they say, "Can you just send me the price?", you say:
- "Let's schedule a quick meeting so I can walk you through the details and make sure this meets your needs. What day and time next week works best for you?"

- This is not about making things easier for you. It is about making sure they understand the full value.

E | Execute Consistently

- No cutting corners. No skipping steps. This is how you sell from now on.
- When you do, your close rate goes up, your sales cycle shortens, and price objections almost disappear.

F | Fuel Others

- Sales is not just about closing deals. It is about helping people make better decisions.
- That includes your prospects and your team.
- If you see another salesperson struggling with discounting or losing deals on price, show them how to sell on value.

Teaching others makes you even better.

Now go sell like a pro.

CHAPTER 11

Turning Resistance Into Revenue

He asked me to build the program that could finally fix it: the revolving door, the missed numbers, the trainees who never ramped.

After three years of watching them burn out or barely break even, he was ready to invest. What he didn't expect was the cost of doing it right.

"Hold on, Wesleyne. Let me pick my jaw off the floor. That number is double what I expected."

I smile. "Totally fair. Let's make sure we're on the same page. Sounds good?"

He nods. "Go ahead."

"You've had sales trainees in your division for three years. Corporate handles product training, but there's no real sales training. Is that right?"

"Yep."

"You realize they're underperforming. Seventy percent leave within a year. The ones who stay generate $150K. That doesn't even cover their cost."

He leans back. That number hits.

I keep going. "If we doubled that revenue, what would that mean?"

He pauses. "We'd finally see a return. We'd actually be profitable."

"And you have the internal resources to fix it?"

"No."

"And if nothing changes?"

"We lose 20 percent of our funding to another department."

I let that land.

Then I ask, "What else do you need from me to get started?"

He doesn't blink. "Wesleyne, I want every single one of my salespeople to sell like you. That was masterful."

That was five years ago. I am still working with that company today, making sure their sales team blows past their quotas every single month.

Objections are a natural part of sales. It is our job to handle them throughout the process rather than let them pop up out of nowhere after we have spent months working with a prospect.

When the VP of Sales pushed back on my price, that was a money objection. He had a number in mind, and mine was double. Instead of backing down or justifying it, I walked him through the gaps in his current program, the financial impact of doing nothing, and the risk to his department.

By the time we finished, price was no longer the issue. The real question was, can we afford not to fix this?

Objections usually fall into four categories: Money, Relationships, Competition, and Timing. The key is not to avoid them but to address them early and steer the conversation toward value. If you wait until the end, you are already on the defensive.

Price Isn't the Problem, Value Is

Objections are a natural part of sales. It is our job to handle them throughout the process, not let them pop up out of nowhere after we have spent months working with a prospect.

When the VP of Sales pushed back on my price, that was a money objection. He had a number in mind, and mine was double. Instead of playing the price game, I brought the conversation back to what actually mattered: the real cost of doing nothing. I walked him through the gaps in his program, the financial impact of inaction, and the long-term risk to his department.

By the time we finished, price was no longer the issue. The real question was, can we afford not to fix this?

Win on price, lose on price. We never let pricing be the reason we win or lose a deal. When a pricing objection comes up, it means one thing: we have not built enough value. That is the cue to walk them back through the problems they shared and remind them what is at stake.

Pricing objections fall into two categories: budget constraints or the price is too high.

Budget constraints mean they have a hard limit on what they can spend, no matter how much value they see. The price is too high, which means they do not see enough value to justify the cost. That is our problem to solve, not theirs.

> *Price isn't the problem, value is.*

Budget and affordability are not the same thing. The budget is what they planned to spend. Affordability is whether they can actually make it work.

In business-to-business sales, affordability is rarely the issue. If a company takes a meeting with us, they can afford some form of our solution. It is just like personal budgeting. Maybe someone set aside $100 for home repairs, but if their air conditioner breaks in the middle of summer, they find the extra $1,000 to fix it.

Businesses work the same way. If they see the value, they will shift money around to invest. That is why early in the sales cycle, we should assess affordability, not just budget.

At the end of the first or second discovery meeting, simply say:

"Our solution ranges from $45,000 to $75,000. Is that in line with your expectations?"

The low end should not be a stripped-down version but a real, viable option. Their response will tell us everything.

If they say yes, we are aligned. If they say they were thinking more like $20,000, we now know there is a gap to address.

The next move is not to defend or justify. Instead, ask:

"Thanks for sharing that. For the right solution, would you be able to increase that number?"

If they say there is no wiggle room, they genuinely cannot afford it, and we move on. But if they say they have some flexibility, we keep the conversation going and keep building value.

At the end of the day, price is never the problem. Perceived value is.

Wrong Contact, Lost Deal

Sales isn't just about your relationship with the prospect. It is about the relationships inside their organization too.

You can have the best pitch, the best product, and the best pricing, but if you are not connected to the right people, your deal is going nowhere.

Your prospect doesn't need to like you. They need to trust you. Trust comes from being a person of your word and providing value. It is as simple as doing what you say you will do when you say you will do it.

Find ways to help them beyond just your product. Maybe they mentioned struggling with running effective team meetings, and you have a great resource on that. Share it. Just because you sell plastic pellets doesn't mean you can't talk about things that matter to them.

Step into their world. Are you tired of hearing that yet? Good. It should be etched in your head.

Listening actively and repeating back what you have heard shows that you care about what matters to them. And by now, you should know the most important person in the sales process: the internal champion.

This is the person who opens doors and makes introductions. They guide you through the internal landscape. They may not sign the contract themselves, but they help you get to the person who does.

If you find yourself in a proposal review meeting and the person across from you says, "I don't have the authority to make the final decision," your mental alarms should start blaring.

It does not mean your champion failed. It means you missed a step.

Your internal champion's job is not to make the decision. Their job is to make sure you are in front of the right people at the right time. If you are not speaking to decision-makers by the time the proposal is being reviewed, you skipped part of the process.

A strong internal champion will tell you how decisions are made, who else needs to be involved, and when to bring them in. That is how you avoid getting stuck or blindsided at the end of the deal.

So, how do you know if you are talking to the right person early on?

If your contact is avoiding conversations about decision-making, not introducing you to the right people, or not advocating for your solution, they are not your champion.

Throughout the sales process, you should be evaluating who else is on the decision-making committee and who has the final sign-off. Asking the right questions early will save you from surprises later:

"Can you walk me through all the steps we need to take to get this approved?"

"Who else would be interested in watching the demo?" (Then follow up with) "Tell me a bit more about that person's role in the organization."

If your main contact isn't making the buying process easier, introducing you to key stakeholders, or giving you insight into how decisions are made, they are not your internal champions. That is your cue to find the right person.

If you realize you are working with the wrong contact, do not keep moving the deal forward. It is on you to get to the right person.

Checklist for Identifying an Internal Champion

- Has influence within the company, even if they are not the final decision-maker.
- Wants the problem solved and is actively working toward a solution.
- Shares insights about the internal decision-making process.
- Introduces you to other stakeholders without you having to ask repeatedly.

The Competitors You Are Ignoring

Most salespeople—to their detriment—only worry about external competition.

Competition falls into two categories: internal and external. Deals are lost just as often to internal competition as they are to direct competitors. Budgets shift. Priorities change. If you are not paying attention, your deal can disappear overnight.

Internal Competition

Every department within a company is fighting for the same pot of money. Budgets may be set at the beginning of the year, but priorities shift. If an emergency pops up or another department under-budgets for a critical need, your prospect's funding can disappear overnight.

Always ensure you are talking to your internal champion. Remember, an internal champion is not just someone who likes you; they are someone who actively moves the deal forward from the inside.

Here is how you know you are working with a true champion:

- They have influence within the company, even if they are not the final decision maker
- They want the problem solved and are actively working toward a solution
- They share insights about how decisions are made internally
- They introduce you to other stakeholders before you have to ask more than once

But how do you spot internal competition before it becomes a problem?

Ask early, "Besides your department, who else is fighting for this budget?"

Dig deeper, "If this doesn't get approved, where else could those funds go?"

Stay ahead. If you hear "budget cuts," ask, "How can we structure this so it still gets approved?"

So when you hear "our budget got cut," don't just walk away. Get curious. Find out how you can get the project approved in the next budget cycle. Better yet, see if you can trim your solution down so they can implement part of it now and the rest later. If you can get your foot in the door, you have won. Also, think creatively. Could your prospect pull funding from another department?

Do Nothing Competitor

The biggest competitor salespeople overlook is the "do nothing" competitor. Sticking with the status quo is always easier than implementing change.

Throughout the sales process, you need to prove that the cost of staying the same is greater than the cost of change. This isn't just about money. It is about time, effort, and return on investment.

How do you handle the "do nothing" competitor?

Make the problem real. Instead of selling your solution, get them to acknowledge the cost of inaction. Ask, "What happens if this problem isn't solved in the next six months?"

Tie pain to urgency. Ask, "How is this issue affecting your team's productivity today?"

Simplify the solution. One of the main reasons we do a five-feature demo is to make change feel simple. If we make the solution look too complex, the prospect will shut down. They will say they don't have time to learn something new, or they won't see the ROI in training their entire team. Never underestimate the time investment they will need to make, but also, never make it look harder than it is. Having a simple ROI calculator in your proposal helps remove this barrier.

External Competition

And of course, everyone keeps an eye out for external competitors. No matter how unique you think your offering is, there is always someone else solving the same problem in a different way. If you have done your competitor analysis, you should know exactly who your top competitors are.

Pay attention to the questions your prospect is asking. Many times, these come directly from a competitor's pitch. They have likely been told that a certain feature or benefit is important, and now they are testing you against it.

Whatever you do, never mention a competitor by name. Your job is to highlight your strengths that you know align with your competitors' weaknesses without calling them out directly. Too many salespeople try to discredit the competition by name, only for the prospect to get curious, do their own research, and end up switching to that competitor instead.

The key to beating the competition is to always assume you are in a competitive deal. Never take your foot off the gas. Stay sharp in your communication. If a prospect starts asking more questions or pushing back, that is your signal to be ready with answers. Not just about what makes you different, but also why your competitors struggle in those areas.

Selling on Their Timeline, Not Yours

Once, I sold an instrument to a patch of dirt.

A large chemical company was in the planning phase of building a new facility in South Texas. I got an inbound inquiry from someone gathering budgetary quotes for the new lab. As we talked, she mentioned they were about two years out from being ready to purchase. Most salespeople would have ended the conversation there. I kept listening.

She also mentioned they had some leftover funds in their budget for the current year.

During our discussion, I casually shared that we would be releasing a new version of the instrument with updated software in a few months. That stopped her in her tracks.

"I want the same instrument that all our facilities have," she said.

I already knew I would get this sale at some point. She had been referred to me by another location that loved working with me and our instruments. It was just a matter of when.

I responded, "I understand. That makes a lot of sense. You have years of historical data and internal expertise with that model."

Then she asked the golden question. "What can you do to help me?"

"Well, you can purchase the instrument now and leave it in the box. I can get special approval from management to delay the start of your warranty until we install it in two years. When you are ready for installation, just give me a call. How does that sound?"

"Oh my goodness, Wesleyne. That sounds amazing. Thank you so much for your help."

That instrument sat in a warehouse for two years while the facility was being built. The company hadn't even broken ground when I received the order.

Timing and internal competition go hand in hand.

Inside every company, there are competing priorities. Your solution may be important, but not urgent compared to everything else on their plate. Other departments are pushing their own agendas. Budgets are being pulled in different directions. Even if your contact wants to move forward, they might get overruled or delayed by something louder or more politically sensitive.

How soon a prospect is ready to buy is none of your business. Stop trying to force people to place an order just because it is the end of the quarter or the end of the year. That is selfish selling. It shifts the focus from being customer-centric and problem-focused to being self-centered and quota-chasing.

At some point in your sales process, you need to understand their timeline. But don't ask, "When do you need to place an order?" or

"When do you plan on making a decision?" I hate those questions. I'm sure they do too.

Instead, ask:

- "Based on what we have discussed, what is your ideal date to have these problems resolved?"
- "When do you need to have your new product up and running?"
- "Are there other processes, people, or departments that need this solution in place before moving forward with their projects?"

Ask when they want their problems fixed, then back-calculate your delivery and implementation timeline to ensure everything aligns. Your job is to be in sync with their goals, not to force a sale.

For example, if a prospect says they need plant upgrades completed by the end of the third quarter, and you know it will take six weeks for delivery and four weeks for implementation (a total of ten weeks), then your response should be:

"Thanks for sharing when the upgrades need to be completed. Based on what you told me, we will need to kick off your project during the last week of April to ensure we meet your deadline. How does that sound?"

If they say yes, you have just gotten a soft verbal commitment. You have inserted yourself into their world and assumed the sale without being sleazy.

If they say no, that is your cue to dig deeper. Maybe they actually want it in place by the first week of June instead. Maybe they won't have funding until the beginning of the third quarter and didn't realize how long implementation would take.

Timing is a conversation, not a dealbreaker.

Sales is not about forcing a close. It is about understanding the prospect's reality and aligning with their needs. When you do that, you don't have to push for a sale. The sale happens naturally.

Now, let's address the real challenge. How do you stay engaged when a deal is months or years away?

Most salespeople lose deals because they lose contact. They check in once every few months with the same tired question: "Just checking in to see if you're ready to move forward." That is lazy selling.

Instead, provide value-driven touchpoints that keep you top of mind:

- Send relevant industry updates that impact their business.
- Share case studies of companies in similar situations and how they solved the same problems.
- Offer a refresher demo when new stakeholders get involved.
- If a competitor launches something new, proactively explain how your solution stacks up before they ask.

Keeping a deal alive is not about following up; it is about making sure your prospect sees you as a resource, not just a salesperson.

By being valuable, you stay in the deal.

Objections will always come up in a deal. It is your job to handle them throughout the sales process and not let them derail it.

By now, you should be a rockstar salesperson with a pipeline full of well-qualified prospects moving through the sales cycle. But here is the real question: Are you working your entire territory effectively, or are you just sticking to the easy wins in your backyard?

You are a field salesperson. Get in the field and sell.

Next up, we are diving into territory planning because a full pipeline means nothing if you are not maximizing every opportunity in your market.

BELIEF Selling™ in Action: Handling Objections with Confidence

B | Break Barriers

- Stop avoiding objections. Address them early so they don't derail the deal later.
- Challenge the belief that objections mean rejection. They signal that value hasn't been established.
- Push past surface-level objections by asking follow-up questions to uncover the real concern.

E | Embrace Growth

- Price is never the real objection. It's a lack of perceived value. Shift the focus to ROI.
- Relationships matter, but trust outweighs likability. Build credibility through consistency and expertise.
- Competition is always in play. Sell your strengths without attacking competitors directly.

L | Learn Skills

- Track common objections and how you overcome them so you can refine your approach.
- Pay attention to where in the sales process objections arise. That tells you what needs to be reinforced earlier.
- Study your market and competitors so you can anticipate and proactively handle objections.

I | Implement Boldly

- When a price objection comes up, walk them through the cost of doing nothing instead of justifying the price.
- If a prospect won't introduce you to other decision-makers, ask, "How do you typically evaluate solutions like this?"
- When they hesitate on timing, ask, "What happens if this problem isn't solved in the next six months?"

E | Execute Consistently

- Address objections throughout the sales process, not just at the close.
- Tie every response back to measurable business impact, not just features or benefits.
- Practice objection handling regularly so you can respond with confidence in the moment.

F | Fuel Others

- Share successful objection-handling techniques with your team. If something works, don't keep it to yourself.
- Role-play common objections to strengthen your ability to navigate them in real conversations.
- Teach new reps that objections are part of the process, not a reason to walk away.

CHAPTER 12

Mastering Your Territory: From Surviving to Thriving

At the end of 2014, I was on top of the world.

Not only had I given birth to a whole human and taken six weeks off to care for him, but I also ended the year as the number two salesperson in my division. And if we are being honest, I still consider myself number one because I hit 125 percent of my annual quota in just 46 weeks.

Being based in Houston, most of my business came from large oil companies. In 2014, oil was trading at over $100 a barrel. My top clients were printing money, scrambling to innovate, and keeping up with refinery demands. Business was booming.

Then, in the middle of the year, one of my top clients dropped a bombshell. He told me the bubble was going to burst.

I had no clue what he meant, so he broke it down for me. The market conditions were not sustainable. Just as fast as oil had skyrocketed, it was about to come crashing down.

By the fourth quarter, I saw it firsthand. My biggest prospects were rushing to place orders before their 2015 budgets were slashed. And then the crash hit.

Every day, I opened my computer to headlines of another oil company laying people off or shutting down production. My pipeline evaporated overnight.

How do you ask someone about a project when half their division just got laid off?

It was brutal. I still remember the gut punch of seeing email after email bounce back. Nearly 50 percent of my contacts were gone. My company did not care that my pipeline had dried up. I had a quota, and they expected me to execute. Period.

So I did what any good salesperson should do. I stopped panicking and started researching.

I realized that while oil was tanking, plastics and asphalt were booming. These industries relied on byproducts of crude oil. With oil prices down, their raw materials were cheaper than ever. That meant higher profits and more demand.

At that moment, I knew I had to flip my customer base. I could not rely on oil anymore. I needed plastics and asphalt clients.

So I got to work.

For the first half of 2015, I spent every week in front of brand-new prospects, learning from existing customers, and showing up at industry events where my new targets would be.

And it paid off.

In less than a year, I flipped my entire customer base. I went from 80 percent of my orders coming from big oil to only 35 percent. Not only did I pull off that pivot, I was named Salesperson of the Year in 2015.

How did I do it?

I did not sit in my office complaining. I did not waste time cold-calling and getting discouraged when no one answered.

Instead, I got in front of the right people. I covered my territory geographically and by industry more effectively than ever before.

And that is exactly what you need to do, whether you are crushing your quota or struggling to hit your numbers. If you are ignoring parts of your territory, chances are your competitors are too. That is an opportunity waiting to be claimed.

So go claim it.

Building a Smarter Territory Strategy

Your territory is like your own small business. You will get out of it what you put into it. If you only focus on the deals that are within reach, you will only ever achieve success that is within reach.

I learned early on that untapped potential exists in places most salespeople ignore. When I visited one of those blink-and-you'll-miss-it towns, where the biggest employer in the city was the company I was calling on, people lit up. I would hear,

> *Building a smarter territory strategy starts with knowing where you can actually win.*

"We have never had a vendor take us to lunch." Or "No one ever comes to visit us."

These were golden opportunities my competitors had completely overlooked. Why? Because most salespeople take the path of least resistance. They go where it is easy and familiar.

That is exactly why territory planning matters. If you are just reacting to whatever comes your way, you are leaving money on the table. You need a plan that puts you in the right places, in front of the right people, at the right time.

Step 1: Start with Your Existing Customers

Why This Matters

Your existing customers hold the key to your next sale. They already see value in what you offer, and they reveal patterns that can help you find more prospects just like them.

What Happens When You Ignore This?

I have seen sales reps who are constantly chasing new business, hoping that cold calls and prospecting alone will build their pipeline. But the truth is, there is often low-hanging fruit right in front of you in the form of existing customers who could buy more, refer you to others, or introduce you to different divisions within their company.

It is frustrating to feel like you are always starting from scratch, but when you slow down and analyze your current customers, you will see a roadmap to where your next wins will come from.

The Right Way to Approach It

Take a step back and analyze:

- Where is my highest concentration of customers?
- What industries are they in?
- What size are they? (Revenue, employee count, market influence)
- What products or services have they purchased?

If you are new to your role, look at where your predecessor had success. Where did they win the most? More importantly, where did they struggle? Understanding those lessons upfront can save you months of wasted effort.

Step 2: Find the Common Thread

Why This Matters

Success leaves clues. Your best customers likely share common traits. If you can identify what connects them, you can replicate success with similar accounts.

What Happens When You Ignore This?

It is easy to think, "I'll sell to anyone who will buy." But that approach makes sales harder than necessary. Without a clear target, you will waste time on the wrong prospects—ones that are never going to buy no matter how great your pitch is.

I worked with a rep once who had a ton of activity but was struggling to close deals. He was frustrated and exhausted. Once we took a closer look, we realized he was spending too much time on the wrong types of prospects. When he shifted his focus to companies that looked like his best customers, his close rate tripled.

The Right Way to Approach It

Look for common threads among your best customers:

- Industry type (Are most of your customers in manufacturing, energy, healthcare, etc.?)
- Company size (Do you sell better to mid-market companies or large enterprises?)
- Product fit (Have you sold the same product line across multiple accounts?)

When you see a pattern, lean into it.

Step 3: Prioritize Where to Spend Your Time

Why This Matters

You only have so many hours in the day, and not all prospects are created equal. If you do not prioritize the right ones, you will run yourself into the ground without seeing real results.

What Happens When You Ignore This?

I have seen reps who work insanely hard but never seem to break through. They are constantly on the road, chasing leads, making calls, and sending emails—but nothing sticks. The problem is not effort. The problem is focus.

When you are spread too thin, everything feels like an uphill battle. It is frustrating and exhausting. But when you focus on the right 20 percent of accounts, you will find that doors start opening, conversations move faster, and deals close with less resistance.

The Right Way to Approach It

Use the 80/20 Rule:

80 percent of your revenue will likely come from 20 percent of your accounts.

Find the right 20 percent and prioritize them.

Ask yourself:

- Which accounts have the biggest revenue potential?
- Who is most likely to buy in the next 6-12 months?
- Where do I already have a strong relationship that I can leverage?

This is about working smarter, not harder.

Turning Strategy into Action

Step 4: Plan Your Travel Like a Pro

Why This Matters

Your time on the road is one of your biggest investments. If you do not plan wisely, you will end up burned out and running in circles instead of closing deals.

What Happens When You Ignore This?

It can be quite tempting to just go where the action is. But without a travel plan, you will end up exhausted, spending hours in the car or airport, wondering where all your time went. I have seen reps waste days driving to one-off meetings that could have been clustered together.

> *Turning strategy into action separates the planners from the closers.*

It is frustrating to put in that much effort and still feel like you are behind.

The Right Way to Approach It

It's not just about how many meetings you schedule—it's about how intentional you are with each one. Focus on quality first. Prioritize meetings that move the deal forward or strengthen the relationship. Once that's clear, then you can layer in the strategy to make your travel more efficient.

- Cluster Your Meetings: If you are traveling to Dallas for a key meeting, schedule three to five additional visits in the area.
- Plan in Advance: The best reps have their travel mapped out weeks in advance.
- Balance Rural vs. Urban Visits:
    - Urban areas: Stack as many meetings as possible.
    - Rural areas: Go deeper with fewer but more meaningful visits.

Step 5: Expand Beyond the Obvious

Why This Matters

Your biggest wins often come from the opportunities others ignore.

What Happens When You Ignore This?

I have seen reps stick to the same safe list of prospects for years. Meanwhile, their competitors are finding new industries, new applications, and new customers and eating up market share as a result.

It is heart-wrenching to watch deals go to someone else just because you did not take the time to explore beyond the obvious.

The Right Way to Approach It

Look for adjacent industries that might have similar needs.

Ask your current customers for introductions to others in their network.

Step 6: Execute with Discipline

Why This Matters

A plan means nothing if you do not implement it.

What Happens When You Ignore This?

I have seen reps put together a great territory plan but never follow through. Then a few months later, they are in panic mode because their pipeline has dried up.

It is frustrating to know what to do but still feel like you are struggling.

The Right Way to Approach It

- Review your calendar weekly to stay on track.
- Block time for travel and prospecting so it does not get pushed aside.
- Be proactive instead of waiting for inbound leads.

Taking Full Ownership of Your Territory

Planning your territory is just the beginning. The real difference comes from how consistently you execute. The best salespeople do not just work hard; they work with purpose and direction.

> *Taking full ownership of your territory changes everything.*

You have done the work to map out your best opportunities. Now it is time to put that plan into action.

Final Thoughts: Own Your Territory, Own Your Success

Your territory is not just a list of accounts; it is an ecosystem of opportunities waiting to be uncovered. The effort you put into planning, prioritizing, and executing will determine how much you get out of it.

You have two choices: you can react to whatever comes your way or take control and create the results you want.

Look at your territory with fresh eyes and ask yourself:

- Where have I been coasting?
- Where have I been overlooking potential?
- Where do I need to step up and take action?

Success is not about luck. It is about being intentional. So go take charge, work smarter and own your territory.

BELIEF Selling™ in Action: Taking Control of Your Territory

B | Break Barriers

- Stop believing that your territory is fixed. It is yours to shape and expand.
- Challenge assumptions about which accounts have the most potential. Look beyond the obvious.
- Pivot when needed. If one industry slows down, find another that is thriving.

E | Embrace Growth

- See your territory as your business, not just a list of accounts. You control the outcome.
- Shift from reactive to proactive. Do not wait for opportunities—create them.
- Focus on what is possible, not what is difficult. Every territory has untapped potential.

L | Learn Skills

- Study your accounts to find patterns in wins and losses. Success leaves clues.
- Research industry trends to identify where the money is flowing in your region.
- Ask your top customers for insights. They know where the next opportunities are.

I | Implement Boldly

- Get in front of the right people. A solid plan means nothing if you do not take action.
- Do not let fear hold you back. Enter new industries and go after accounts your competitors ignore.
- Take at least one bold action this week—visit a new region, target a new industry, or expand your reach.

E | Execute Consistently

- Block time each week for territory planning. If it is not scheduled, it will not happen.
- Stick to your plan, but adjust when needed. The best salespeople analyze and adapt.
- Cover all parts of your territory, not just the ones that are easiest to visit.

F | Fuel Others

- Share territory insights with your team. What you learn can help others win too.
- If a strategy works for you, teach it to someone else. Helping others reinforces your mastery.
- Build relationships in every industry you serve. The more you give, the more doors open.

CHAPTER 13

Bet on Yourself

When we started this journey, I told you about my first international sales meeting in Germany. What I didn't tell you was that I was the only Black person in the room and one of just five women in a sea of thousands.

I remember looking around, my stomach in knots, and thinking:

"There's no way I'm going to be successful. I don't belong here. I have no experience. No one here looks like me. No one here is going to take me seriously."

I had no sales training. No mentors. No roadmap. But I did have one thing—a decision to make.

I could either let that doubt swallow me whole, or I could prove myself wrong.

I chose to bet on myself—a decision that changed my entire life.

That scrappy young woman—the one who doubted herself in that conference room—went on to close millions of dollars in business and impact thousands of salespeople by teaching them how to win.

A salesperson I hired over a decade ago recently told me something that stopped me in my tracks. Over lunch, he shared how he had passed on one of my lessons to a colleague. Then he looked me in the eye and said, "Last year, I paid more in taxes than my entire salary before I started working for you."

That is what happens when you commit to growth. That is what happens when you stop sitting on the sidelines of your life and start playing to win.

The Difference Between Winning and Quitting

If you have made it this far, you have read every page. But reading is not enough. If you do not take action, nothing changes.

Take the loss and find a way to win next time. Every setback is a setup for a comeback.

Miss your quota? Use that fire to execute your prospecting plan.

Get out of your office. Go see people. Have real conversations.

Stop making excuses. Instead of saying why you cannot, start mapping out how you can.

I believe in you. But the real question is, do you believe in yourself?

This career does not tolerate the weak. It is lonely in the field. You will lose more than you win. You will have days when you question everything.

> ***Success starts with action.***

Most people quit in those moments.

And that is exactly why most people never become great.

What separates a truly successful salesperson from an average one is neither talent nor luck. It is the number of times you get back up after being knocked down.

Everything you have learned in this book will not work perfectly the first time you try it. That is not a sign to quit. That is a sign to go back, reread, refine, and execute again.

And again.

And *again*.

The more reps you put in, the greater your success.

And if you ever feel like you do not belong in this world of sales, I want you to remember this.

I once stood in a room where I felt like an outsider. I once doubted whether I had what it took.

But I made a choice.

And now, it is time for you to make yours.

Success Starts With Action

This is not goodbye. It is just the beginning of your next level.

I want to see you win. I want to hear about your breakthroughs, your big deals, and your transformations. And I want you to be surrounded by other sales professionals who are just as committed to mastering customer-centric, problem-focused selling.

That is why I created a space for people like you. A place where we share wins, troubleshoot challenges, and push each other to higher levels.

Do not do this alone. Join us here: yoursalesreset.com.

You have spent time learning. Now it is time to apply.

In the next 24 hours, take one step and reach out to a new prospect.

Revisit a lost deal.

Refine your pitch.

Start the exercise from the chapter that challenged you the most.

Action beats hesitation every single time.

You already have everything you need. Now go make it happen.

I am rooting for you.

APPENDIX

Tools to Put BELIEF Selling™ Into Action

This book wasn't meant to be just read; it was meant to be used.

The following worksheets, guides, and templates are designed to help you turn insight into action. Each one connects directly to a chapter in *The Sales Reset* and gives you a structured, practical way to apply what you've learned.

Whether you're planning a tough conversation, writing your next email, or preparing for a big proposal, these tools are here to guide you back to clarity.

You don't need more noise; you need structure, intention, and a way to move forward with confidence.

Tools are only as good as the beliefs behind them.

Let's get to work.

Want a digital copy with even more worksheets and templates?

Download the full BELIEF Selling™ Toolkit at **www.yoursalesreset.com**.

Centering Sales Affirmations

Referenced in: Chapter 1—Entering the Mysterious World of Sales

Before you start prospecting, leading a call, or walking into a proposal meeting, center yourself. These affirmations are designed to ground your mindset in truth, clarity, and purpose. No pressure. No pretending. Just presence.

You don't need to say them all. Pick one that speaks to you today. Speak it out loud. Let it settle in.

Sales Affirmations

- I don't have to prove my worth. I already have it
- I lead with clarity, not control
- I ask questions because I care, not because I'm unsure
- I trust that the right clients will recognize the value I bring
- I was chosen for this moment. I don't have to earn my seat
- I sell solutions, not myself
- I can slow down without losing momentum
- I do not chase. I connect
- Rejection is not personal. It's information
- I let go of needing to be perfect. I just need to be present
- I do hard things without hardening myself
- I lead with empathy, not ego
- My voice matters in this room
- I've handled bigger deals than this. I can handle this too
- I don't need every deal. I need the right ones
- I ask with confidence because I've done the work
- I create space for real conversation, not just transactions
- I'm not here to convince. I'm here to serve
- Silence is not rejection. It's space to reflect
- I show up fully even when the outcome is uncertain

Try this: Pick one affirmation each week. Write it at the top of your planner. Say it before a call. Repeat it after a tough moment. Let it shape how you show up in every conversation.

BELIEF Selling™ Journal Prompts

Referenced in: Chapter 1—Entering the Mysterious World of Sales

Use these prompts to check in with yourself weekly. They're not about performance. They're about presence.

When you slow down and ask better questions of yourself, you show up stronger for others.

Weekly Journal Prompts

- What am I holding back from saying in my sales conversations, and why?
- Where am I overexplaining instead of trusting that I've done enough?
- What recent challenge showed me how much I've grown?
- When did I feel most confident this week? What led to that moment?
- What pattern keeps showing up in my deals, and what is it teaching me?
- Who am I when I'm not trying to prove myself?
- What's one belief I have about myself that's getting in the way of my success?
- What do I want to be known for by the people I sell to?
- Where am I showing up out of fear instead of purpose?
- What would change if I stopped selling to be liked and started selling to serve?
- Where do I feel misaligned in how I sell vs. who I really am?
- What does a "win" look like this week beyond just closing a deal?
- When I get discouraged, what truth do I need to come back to?
- What would it look like to lead every call with curiosity, not control?
- What part of my story do I need to remember today?

Reminder: You don't have to answer all of them every week. Start with the one that hits your heart the hardest. That's your invitation to flow.

Writing Your Story Exercise

Referenced in: Chapter 1—Entering the Mysterious World of Sales

Use this worksheet to reconnect with the moments that shaped who you are today. Your story isn't a detour, it's your foundation.

Step-by-Step Instructions

1. Set a timer for 20 minutes.
   Let your mind flow. Don't filter. Don't judge.

2. On a blank sheet of paper, list every pivotal moment in your life. Include highs, lows, risks, wins, failures anything that changed you. Here are a few questions to get you going:
   - What moment in your life felt like a turning point?
   - When were you scared but took the leap anyway?
   - When did something not go as planned but lead you to a better outcome?
   - What did you walk away from that made you stronger?
   - When did you feel most proud of who you were becoming?

3. Read your list out loud.
   Hearing your own voice helps your nervous system register the truth of your journey.

4. Choose the top 3 moments that shaped your strength the most. Mark them with a star.

5. For each of the 3 moments, answer the following:
   - What happened?
   - What did I learn?
   - How has this helped me in sales or life?

6. Write your new internal belief:
   - Example: "Because I've lived through that, I know I can handle this.

Want Structure?
Download the printable version of this exercise at [www.yoursalesreset.com/story]

Funnel Quick Reference Guide — BELIEF Selling™ Reset

Referenced in: Chapter 4—From Chaos to Consistency

This is your structured sales process—the cure to your random acts of selling. Each stage is intentional, and each one can be shaped by belief or blocked by doubt. Use this table to spot where your mindset may be affecting execution and reframe with a BELIEF Selling™ reset.

> *Each stage is intentional, and each one can be shaped by belief or blocked by doubt.*

Stage	What's Happening	Belief That Creeps In	BELIEF Selling™ Reset
1. Identify	You're determining if a lead is MQL or SQL and trying to assess intent, but you're hesitant to engage or disqualify.	I don't want to waste time or miss an opportunity.	Break Barriers: I trust my process. Every 'no' clears space for a better 'yes'.
2. Nurture	You're uncovering real problems, getting the right people involved, checking budget and timing, but you hesitate to go deep.	If I ask too many questions, they'll back off.	Elevate Mindset: I'm here to understand their world. Depth builds trust.
3. Demo (if needed)	You're tempted to show every feature instead of sticking to five tied directly to their problems.	If I don't show enough, they won't see the value.	Learn Skillset: Less impresses more. Align every feature to a real pain point.

4. Proposal	You're tempted to email a quote and wait instead of scheduling a live proposal review to walk through their issues and listen for the micro-yes.	They'll come back if they're serious.	Implement Boldly: No more hoping. I lead the conversation until the close.
5. Close	You've got a verbal yes but hesitate to ask directly or handle final objections.	I don't want to blow it by pushing too soon.	Execute Consistently: If they said yes, I follow through with confidence and clarity.

SWOT Example

Referenced in: Chapter 5—Building Your Competitive Edge

You can't lead the market without first understanding where you stand. This worksheet helps you get clear on what sets you apart, where you need to grow, and how to spot the gaps your competitors are leaving wide open. Be honest. Be specific. Then go sell with confidence.

Sample Company SWOT Analysis

Strengths (Internal)

- Fast technical support response times
- Strong industry knowledge among sales team
- Streamlined customer onboarding process
- Deep relationships with academic and R&D clients

Weaknesses (Internal)

- Outdated website with limited product information
- Long lead times for special order items
- Inconsistent follow-up after demo requests
- Low visibility at industry trade shows

Opportunities (External)

- New product launch in corrosion-resistant coatings
- Increase sales in under-served western territory
- Cross-sell to labs currently using only service contracts
- Partner with local engineering schools for visibility

Threats (External)

- Two new low-cost competitors entering your region
- Supply chain disruptions from overseas suppliers
- Shifting customer expectations for sustainability metrics
- Competitor acquiring key accounts through bundling

Competitive Analysis Sample

Referenced in: Chapter 5—Building Your Competitive Edge

Before you can position yourself effectively in the field, you need to understand who else is in the room. This example will show you how to break down your competitors' strengths and weaknesses using real data, not guesses. Use this format to guide your own analysis.

Competitor Name: PrecisionTech Instruments

Market Position: Known for low pricing and wide product catalog

Step 1—What they say about themselves

Review their About Us page, brochures, and LinkedIn profile.

- "Industry leader in budget-friendly solutions for basic testing needs"

- "Rapid delivery across all US regions"
- "Engineered for simplicity and efficiency"

Step 2—What customers and employees say

Check Google Reviews, Glassdoor, and forums.

- Customers report poor post-sale service and lack of application support
- Employee reviews mention high turnover in technical support roles
- "Great for the price, but we had to troubleshoot on our own"

Step 3—What the market says

Review their social media and customer engagement.

- Social posts focus on deals and promotions, little educational content
- Engagement is low: few comments, little interaction
- One prospect said, "They were responsive until we signed, then crickets"

Competitive Strengths (compared to your company):

- Broad product line covers basic testing needs
- Competitive pricing that appeals to budget-conscious customers
- Fast shipping for standard items

Competitive Weaknesses (compared to your company):

- Poor post-sale technical support and training
- Lack of customization or consultative selling
- High employee turnover affecting customer experience
- Low engagement and visibility with technical decision-makers online

Your Opportunity to Win

- Lead with your personalized service and deep application knowledge
- Emphasize field support and troubleshooting that starts before the sale and continues after the install
- Highlight your ability to align solutions to customer-specific needs, not just sell products

Pain–Problem–Impact Mapping Table

Referenced in: Chapter 7—The Power of Impact: Turning Problems Into Opportunities

When you're in the field, you're not just hearing what's wrong, you're seeing it. This table helps you connect what your buyer says to what's really happening behind the scenes, and how it's impacting their business and their life.

"When you tie your solution to a clear, undeniable impact, you're not just selling. You're solving something that matters." ~ Wesleyne

Pain (What They Say)	Problem (What's Really Going On)	Impact (Why It Matters—Business + Personal)
"We keep missing delivery deadlines."	Poor production scheduling or bottlenecks in raw material flow	Strained distributor relationships, lost orders, plant manager working weekends
"We're running too many quality checks."	Lack of trust in suppliers or inconsistent material performance	Downtime increases, scrap rates rise, ops leader under pressure from execs
"My team won't follow the new process."	Change wasn't communicated clearly or doesn't match workflow	Productivity drop, frustration on the floor, shift leads venting during huddles

"We're losing customers to the competition."	Tech is outdated or reps aren't trained on value differentiation	Sales leader questioned by regionals, loss of confidence in solution quality
"Purchasing won't approve anything new."	Finance doesn't see ROI or internal champion lacks influence	Deal stalls, sales cycle drags out, your contact looks powerless internally
"The rep from X company is here every week."	Competitor is building stickiness while you're playing catch-up	You're losing mindshare, share-of-wallet, and potentially, the whole account

Warm Emailing Guide

Referenced in: Chapter 8—Mastering Prospecting: Turning Effort Into Results

This guide will help you build cold emails that feel personal, confident, and customer-focused. Use it to open real conversations, not just fill your pipeline. These examples are tailored to what your buyers face every day.

Subject Line Principles

- Keep it short (under 6 words)
- Avoid gimmicks or bait-and-switch
- Use curiosity or relevance, not pressure
- Examples:
  - Cut lab calibration delays?
  - Reducing inspection backlog at scale
  - For your field reps in [Region]

Opening Line: Earn Attention

- Tie to something real:
    - A product recall
    - A compliance challenge
    - A missed shipment or backorder trend
- Example:
  Saw your update on lead times. Many field leaders I work with are seeing the same and rethinking their forecasting inputs.

Anchor to Their Reality (Not Your Pitch)

- Highlight a specific problem you solve
- Use language that matches their role
- Frame it with empathy, not assumptions
- Example:
  Plant managers keep telling me their reps struggle to qualify opportunities early leading to long sales cycles and missed targets.

Introduce Yourself with Purpose

Keep it one line. Focus on the value you bring, not your credentials.

Example:

I support field teams in packaging and industrial supply to shorten time-to-close and boost deal quality with less rep burnout.

Call to Action: Low Pressure, Clear Ask

- Offer a short call or resource
- Make it feel optional but valuable
- Examples:
    - Want a quick checklist that's working for other industrial reps?
    - Open to a 10-minute call to share what's moved the needle for your peers?

Warm Email Checklist

- Is this email relevant to their role?
- Did I speak to a real problem or opportunity?
- Is it under 150 words?
- Would you reply to it yourself?

DIVE DEEP Discovery™ Questioning Framework

Referenced in: Chapter 9—Mastering the Art of Discovery

Sales conversations should feel like clarity, not interrogation. The DIVE DEEP Discovery™ Framework helps you guide conversations with curiosity, empathy, and purpose so you uncover what matters most before recommending any solution.

Use this quick guide during discovery calls to ground your questions and stay focused on what your buyer is experiencing. Remember, you don't need to ask every question and there is no specific order you have to ask questions in.

D—Dig for What's Below the Surface

Purpose: Get past surface-level symptoms. Find the hidden blockers, expectations, and tensions that might be unspoken.

Ask:

- What's happening today that you didn't expect when this year started?
- I noticed [observation]. What's behind that?
- Where are things starting to feel stuck?

I—Investigate the Process

Purpose: Understand what's actually happening in the day-to-day. Look for bottlenecks, miscommunication, and handoffs.

Ask:

- Can you walk me through how that usually goes?

- What tends to get skipped or delayed in this process?
- How does this work when everything goes right and when it doesn't?

V—Validate the Impact

Purpose: Create urgency without pressure. This is how you help them see the cost of inaction.

Ask:

- What happens when this doesn't get fixed?
- How has this shown up in production, efficiency, or customer feedback?
- Who else is affected when this happens?

E—Echo What You Heard

Purpose: Build trust, show active listening, and clarify alignment.

Say:

- You mentioned that [problem] is creating [impact]. Did I capture that fully?
- Sounds like [summary]. Is that the full picture, or is there more behind it?

Best Practices:

- Talk less than 30 percent of the time
- Ask follow-up questions instead of rushing to pitch
- Use your notes to mirror language back to the buyer
- Avoid yes/no questions except when Echoing

Sell the Solution, Not the Sticker Price

Referenced in: Chapter 10—Stop Selling on Price, Start Selling on Value

Your proposal is not just a document. It's a conversation. A chance to prove you were listening and to lead your prospect toward a confident decision.

Use this to prepare before sending or delivering any proposals.

Step 1. Recap Their Problems

- Start with what they told you. Pull directly from your discovery notes.
- What were the 2 to 3 most pressing problems they shared?
- What language did they use to describe them?
- Examples:
  - They're experiencing 27 hours/month of lost production due to shift change delays.
  - Engineers use inconsistent design processes leading to rework and missed timelines.

Step 2. Map Problems to Solutions

Show how each problem connects directly to your offer. Keep it simple and client-focused. Have at least 3, but no more than five problems and solutions.

- Problem → Our Solution
- Problem → Our Solution
- Problem → Our Solution
- Examples:
  - Problem: Inconsistent design workflows → Solution: Standardized design checklist module
  - Problem: Shift downtime → Solution: Remote log-in/log-out system

How does this solve what matters most to them?

Step 3. Validate the Fit

Before you hit send or start your review meeting, ask yourself:

- ☐ Does this proposal solve their most important issue?
- ☐ Is it clear how each part ties back to their world?
- ☐ Have I scheduled a time to walk them through it live?

Step 4. Call-to-Action Language

Here's how to verbally ask for the sale with clarity and confidence:

- "Based on what we've covered, are you ready to move forward?"
- "Is there anything else you need to feel confident saying yes?"

Step 5. Keep It Conversational

Quick checklist to guide your tone:

- ☐ I'm showing, not telling
- ☐ I'm guiding, not pushing
- ☐ I'm tying price to value, not features
- ☐ I'm treating the proposal as a partnership

Acknowledgments

Writing this book has been a journey filled with challenges, growth, and countless moments of inspiration. It would not have been possible without the support, guidance, and encouragement of so many people who have walked alongside me through this process.

First and foremost, I thank God for giving me the strength, wisdom, and perseverance to bring this book to life. His grace has carried me through every obstacle and moment of doubt.

To my boys, William and Wesley. You are my greatest joy and my biggest motivation. Watching you grow into incredible young men inspires me daily. Every late night, every early morning, and every ounce of effort I put into this book was driven by my desire to show you that with faith, hard work, and perseverance, anything is possible. I hope this book is a reminder to always chase your dreams, push past challenges, and believe in the impact you can make in this world. I love you more than words can express.

To my family, your unwavering love and belief in me has been my foundation. Your encouragement, prayers, and patience has meant everything.

To my friends and mentors who have spoken life into me, challenged my thinking, and reminded me of my purpose. Thank you for being my sounding board and my source of wisdom. Your words and actions have shaped me in ways you may never fully realize.

To every sales professional I have had the privilege of coaching, mentoring, and learning from. This book is for you. Your stories, struggles, and victories have fueled my passion and given me the inspiration to create something that truly serves you.

To my team and those who have supported me behind the scenes. You are the unsung heroes. From helping me refine my thoughts to ensuring every detail of this book came together, I appreciate you more than words can express.

And finally, to the reader. Thank you for taking this journey with me. My hope is that these pages equip you, challenge you, and ultimately help you step into the best version of yourself as a sales professional and as a person.

About the Author

Wesleyne Whittaker is a powerhouse sales strategist, keynote speaker, and coach who transforms field sales teams from struggling to unstoppable. With over 15 years of experience in field sales leadership, she has mastered the art of turning technical professionals into top-performing salespeople. As a Fascinate Certified Advisor and the founder of Transformed Sales, Wesleyne equips sales leaders with the tools, strategies, and confidence to drive revenue and build high-performing teams.

Wesleyne is known for her no-nonsense, results-driven approach to sales that prioritizes problem solving, connection, and a deep understanding of the customer's world over scripts and pressure. In *The Sales Reset*, she introduces BELIEF Selling™, her proven framework designed to help sales professionals overcome self-limiting beliefs, shift into an empowered mindset, and sell with boldness and consistency. Unlike traditional sales books that focus solely on tactics, this book goes deeper by challenging the internal mindset barriers that often derail performance while offering step-by-step practical strategies that can be applied immediately. It is built for salespeople who want real results, not just theories.

Beyond sales, Wesleyne is deeply passionate about mentorship, personal growth, and faith. She is the founder of a nonprofit dedicated to supporting women who have experienced abusive relationships.

When she's not coaching sales teams or writing, you'll find Wesleyne enjoying a gluten-free meal (with no zucchini in sight), leading transformative discussions, or empowering others to reach their full potential.

Connect with Wesleyne:

LinkedIn: www.linkedin.com/in/wesleyne

Website: transformedsales.com

Thank You for Reading My Book! Can You Do Me a Quick Favor?

I appreciate you taking the time to read The Sales Reset. My goal is to help you break through barriers, solve real problems, and sell smarter.

But I am always looking to make this even better. Your feedback helps me improve this book and every book I write in the future.

Can you take two minutes to leave a review on Amazon?

Tell me what stood out, what worked for you, and even what you would love to see more of. Your review does not just help me. It helps other sales professionals find the book and level up their game.

Thanks for being part of this journey. I appreciate you.

Sell boldly,

Wesleyne Whittaker

www.ingramcontent.com/pod-product-compliance
Lightning Source LLC
LaVergne TN
LVHW020426070526
838199LV00004B/298